Raise Up Off Me

Raise Up Off Me

A Portrait of
Hampton Hawes

*by Hampton Hawes
and Don Asher*

New Introduction by Gary Giddins

A DA CAPO PAPERBACK

Library of Congress Cataloging in Publication Data

Hawes, Hampton, 1928-
  Raise up off me.

  (A Da Capo paperback)
  Reprint of the 1974 ed. published by Coward, McCann
& Geoghegan, New York.
  1. Hawes, Hampton, 1928-   2. Musicians—
Biography. I. Asher, Don, joint author. II. Title.
[ML417.H27A3 1979]   786.1'092'4 [B]   79-15345
ISBN 0-306-80101-9 (pbk.)

ISBN 0-306-80101-9
First Da Capo Paperback Edition 1979

This Da Capo Press paperback edition of *Raise Up Off Me:
A Portrait of Hampton Hawes* is an unabridged
republication of the first edition published by Coward,
McCann and Geoghegan, Inc. in New York in 1974,
supplemented with a new introduction by Gary Giddins.
It is reprinted by arrangement with Don Asher.

Published by Da Capo Press, Inc.
A Subsidiary of Plenum Publishing Corporation
227 West 17th Street, New York, N.Y. 10011

Introduction

Hampton Hawes was playing San Francisco's Both/And club in 1966, when Don Asher dropped by to hear him. That year Asher published his first novel and was playing piano in a comedy revue, while Hawes, one of California's most admired and influential musicians in the '50s, was struggling to revive his career after five years' imprisonment on a heroin bust. Asher introduced himself, remembering a night at Boston's Storyville club more than ten years before, when Hawes's first album was garnering enthusiastic reviews and jazz polls were falling in his lap. Asher "had never heard any pianist crackle and burn up a club like this." Now it was different — Hampton looked tired and the place was practically empty. Asher invited him to the show where he was working and when Hawes walked in a few nights later, they reminisced until dawn. The writer said, "Let's do a book on your life."

The project began in earnest the following year, as the two alternated visits to Los Angeles and San Francisco, and Asher tried to absorb the rhythms and slang of Hampton's voice, discovering unexpected difficulties in making his language ring true. In an article on their collaboration, Asher reported Hampton's response to the preliminary draft of the book. Hawes is the first speaker:

"Do I say 'don't' when I mean 'doesn't' and 'you' when I mean 'you're?'"

"Most of the time. The tone of the book should be conversational rather than literary."

"Okay, but we don't want people to think we're setting them up with deliberate minority group talk. Oh, and don't say John Kennedy 'went down' in Dallas; say 'got killed' or 'was murdered.'"

"I took that phrase straight off the tape."

"I know, but I didn't mean for you to transcribe stuff directly. In this case, it's not dignified enough . . ."

This kind of discussion went on for two weeks before Asher embarked on a second draft. The care put into making the narrative flow, the attention to nuance and rhythmic immediacy, is evident on every page of the finished work. *Raise Up Off Me* is a major contribution to the literature of jazz. It belongs to a small, little-known genre of autobiographical works that not only provide insight into the music and its makers, but also shed light on race relations, Bohemian attitudes toward sex and drugs, alienation, and the predicament of the black artist in America. If novels with jazz settings are always disappointing and often ludicrous (how is it that a native phenomenon with the mythic resonance of jazz should attract so very few of our top writers?), the best of the musicians' own stories fully satisfy the demands of character, place, and language.

Raise Up Off Me was the first book to give an insider's view of the most provocative and misunderstood movement in jazz — the modernism of the '40s, bebop. Sidney Bechet's *Treat It Gentle,* Jelly Roll Morton and Alan Lomax's *Mister Jelly Roll,* Louis Armstrong's *Satchmo,* Mezz Mezzrow and Bernard Wolfe's *Really the Blues,* and Billie Holiday and William Dufty's *Lady Sings the Blues,* although varying greatly in style and veracity, were among the more valuable as-told-to collaborations tracing the development of jazz from Congo Square in New Orleans to Cafe Society in New York. But bebop, that strangely beautiful and tumultuous music long associated in the public mind with rebellion, hipsterism, and narcotics, was all but unspoken for. When Hampton Hawes's story was published in 1974, the only previous oral histories on the subject were Robert Reisner's *Bird: The Legend of Charlie Parker,* an anecdotal montage more concerned, as the subtitle promises, with legend than life, and Charles Mingus's *Beneath the Underdog,* a searing self-examination in which music plays only a peripheral role. For that matter, there have been no others since *Raise Up Off Me,* although books by Dizzy Gillespie and Art Pepper are currently slated for publication.

In his biography of Chopin, James Huneker took as his jumping-off point Flaubert's dictum urging "young writers to lead ascetic lives that in their art they might be violent." I wonder what Huneker would have made of Hampton's dissolute existence, or of the aggrandized hedonism of Charlie Parker, or of that entire generation of musicians for whom Parker was the Messiah and Hawes a prominent disciple. On first consideration, their stories seem to thoroughly confound any link between artistic violence and personal abstinence. Reading of their harrowing, if sometimes hilarious, misadventures in search of a fix, it's difficult to imagine how they summoned forth the energy, strength, and clarity of mind to create so much exquisite music. On closer inspection, their involvement with heroin, though ultimately destructive, seems to have helped them sustain that "psychic violence." Hawes writes of "a tremendous drive to turn inward, stay blind, blot it all out." He expresses political frustrations, but is content to wage his fight through music. Confronted with adversity and even the possibility of his own death, he reveals an utterly passive fatalism. As

Huneker wrote of Chopin, "the bright roughness of adventure was missing from his quotidian existence. The tragedy was within." In the end, Hawes learns that he was already half-dead for twenty years. Yet his music remained impassioned, fiery, violent.

Bebop was more than an onomatopoeically dubbed style of making music; it represented the politicized stance of a generation of young blacks born during the Harlem Renaissance and now confronting an America disjointed by the Second World War. In *Blues People,* Leroi Jones suggested: "Between the Thirties and the end of World War II, there was perhaps as radical a change in the psychological perspective of the Negro American toward America as there was between the Emancipation and 1930." Bebop was the most vivid and eloquent expression of that psychic turmoil. For whites, bebop embodied the lure of nonconformity and provided an instant metaphor of cultural alienation — Norman Mailer's essay, "The White Negro," and Jack Gelber's play, "The Connection," among many works fueled by that metaphor, were more widely discussed in their day than the achievements of Charlie Parker. For Hawes, bop was the ticket out of a preacher's home, where jazz and blues were abominated; the only way he could develop his talent was to sneak practice hours while everyone else was in church.

In *Raise Up Off Me,* Hampton's rebelliousness and increasing bitterness — exacerbated by the tragically premature deaths of everyone he most admires: Parker, Wardell Gray, Sonny Clark, Clifford Brown, Art Tatum, Billie Holiday, and John Kennedy, who granted him executive clemency — is given an acrid twist by his abiding fantasy of being Captain America or, as he puts it, "the Flash Gordon of the niggers." The same young man who boasts of membership in "the first generation to rebel, playing bebop, trying to be different," spent much of his school days doodling "navy

dudes in epaulets, airplanes and pilots in their airforce suntans";
the habitually AWOL junkie soldier who finds solace with a family
of whores, muses, "If the scales had tipped a little to the left I
might have got myself cleaned up and come back a hero, picture on
the cover of *Jet* and *Newsweek (Soldier singlehandedly cements
Orient ties)."* When Art Tatum compliments him, it feels "like the
King telling you you're one of the most loyal and courageous
subjects in the land." He addresses the President from prison as an
"officer in battle informing my commander. . . " His ambivalences
about society and his prospects in it are resolved chiefly by his
absorption in music, and also by the never-neverland of drugs—an
isolation he finally breaks through.

Some people are offended by Hawes's writing about drugs. In
certain quarters, heroin is one of the last taboos, mentioned only in
hushed tones and with embarrassment. The result is an astonish-
ingly small body of work on the subject — far less, for example,
than exists on the relationship between hallucinogens and rock.
But it's been a long time since heroin was part of the jazz scene,
and Hawes's reminiscences are refreshing in their lack of moraliz-
ing and piety. A man resilient enough to defeat a habit that has
devastated his career (but not his talent) has the right to laugh at his
calamities. Frequently, his wit takes the form of pop culture
similes: the army is populated by "Joe Palooka and Clark Kent
types," a lawyer looks like "a 1936 editor of *Batman,"* Tatum
lumbers along like Bela Lugosi, a mysterious Mexican looks "like
a bellboy in one of those W.C. Fields one-reelers." Humor mutes
but doesn't eradicate the bitterness, however, as Hawes's stinging
account of a European tour and its aftermath make clear. Nor can it
disguise his penchant for tortuous self-justification — when he's
leaving his wife for a younger woman, or deciding to make a
"commercial" record. Still, his candor and will to survive com-

mand respect and understanding.

Raise Up Off Me was favorably received on publication, by critics who recognized the gap it filled in jazz writing, or who were simply carried away by the book's vivacity, humor, and authenticity. It won a Deems Taylor-ASCAP award, and spurred renewed interest in Hampton Hawes. Unfortunately, that interest came at a time when the pianist was engaged in a disastrous attempt to make records he thought would appeal to a broader contemporary audience. They weren't distinguished, and Hawes never sounded as comfortable performing on electric keyboards as he did when playing the acoustic piano. It may be useful here to trace his musical development, as documented on recordings.

The first record Hawes listened closely to as a boy was Earl Hines's "Boogie Woogie on St. Louis Blues"; he listened to other classic jazz pianists as well — Fats Waller, Art Tatum, Albert Ammons — until a high school classmate, Eric Dolphy (who became a major force in the jazz avant-garde of the '60s), introduced him to the modern style via Dizzy Gillespie. At nineteen, Hawes found himself working with Charlie Parker in Howard McGhee's band at the Hi-De-Ho club. Parker's influence was immediate and absolute, and Hawes commenced translating the saxophonist's style to the piano. The best examples of Hawes's early work can be found on *The East/West Controversy* (Xanadu 104) and *Wardell Gray Live in Hollywood* (Xanadu 146). Even at this early stage, his playing demonstrates the fiery jubilance, the terse bebop lyricism, and precise fingering one associates with his mature work. He had not yet developed the expressive bluesiness, the gospel chords, tremolos, and walking bass figures for which he would become famous.

Hawes's reputation was made with six albums recorded for Lester Koenig's Contemporary Records in less than a year and a half. First there were three albums by *The Trio* (C3505, C3515, C3523), with bassist Red Mitchell and drummer Chuck Thompson. Then, one evening in November, 1956, the Hampton Hawes Quartet recorded *All Night Session* (C7545, C7546, C7547). It was an unprecedented recording venture, testifying to Hawes's inexhaustible invention when it came to the blues and favorite standards. The clarity of his improvisations and the deep feeling he uncovered set the stage for many of the soul pianists who became prominent in the late '50s, and also influenced many of the more facile keyboard technicians on the West Coast, including Oscar Peterson and the mystifyingly successful Andre Previn. During this period, Hawes also recorded impressively as a sideman, notably with Sonny Rollins (Contemporary 7564) and Charles Mingus (Trip 5017).

His last important recording before his drug bust in late 1958 was *For Real!* (C7589), with saxophonist Harold Land and the exceptional rhythm section of Scott LaFaro and Frank Butler. The album was notable for an imaginative, controlled reading of "Wrap Your Troubles In Dreams," and the pianist's brisk, percussive accompaniment throughout. (Hawes was a gifted accompanist; in 1952, he provided support for a bass solo on Wardell Gray's "Farmer's Market" — see *Central Avenue,* Prestige P-24062 — that was of sufficient melodic interest to inspire lyrics by Annie Ross.) Five years later, he returned to the Contemporary studios to cut one of his finest albums, *The Green Leaves of Summer* (C7614); the title selection is somewhat sentimental, but Hawes's moving rubato introduction and rhythmic middle part give it unsuspected weight. The entire session was vigorously conceived and impeccably performed.

Hawes's best records during the next ten years resulted from live sessions and were released in America years after they were recorded — *The Seance* (C7621) and *I'm All Smiles* (C7631), both from a trio engagement with Red Mitchell in 1966; *The Challenge* (RCA JPL1-1508), an interesting but only partly successful solo album recorded during his 1968 visit to Japan; and two surprisingly lively trio sets from an evening in Copenhagen, *Live at the Montmartre* (Arista 1020) and the much superior, bebop-revisited *A Little Copenhagen Night Music* (Arista 1043).

Raise Up Off Me ends with a determined Hawes marching up to the offices of Fantasy-Prestige with "my new plans, my Afro and my funny clothes," and securing a record contract. Prestige pretty much gave him his head, but the soft-funk recordings alienated his older audience and didn't attract a new one. His playing on them is relatively faceless and uninvolved—interestingly, they went out of print, unlike the acoustic recordings of the Fifties. His marriage to Josie Black didn't last either, and finding work outside of California was almost impossible. He did some studio work, performed with Joan Baez and Seals and Croft, and tried unsuccessfully to finance a tour with guitarist Denny Diaz, of Steely Dan. Hampton decided to return permanently to "wood," his phrase for the acoustic piano. He played extremely well on Charlie Haden's *The Golden Number* (Horizon SP 727) and Art Pepper's *Living Legend* (Contemporary 7633). *Raise Up Off Me* went out of print and when people asked Don Asher how to get a copy, his stock reply was, "You can steal it from the library but I wish you wouldn't."

Hampton Hawes, who often complained that jazz musicians had to die before they were appreciated in America, died of a massive stroke on May 22, 1977. He was forty-eight. His last two albums were posthumously released, and proved to be among his best — the lovely, questing duets with Charlie Haden, *As Long As There's Music* (Artists House 4) and *Hampton Hawes at the Piano* (Contemporary 7637), with a sensational performance of "When I

Grow Too Old To Dream." A club in Los Angeles called the Safari commissioned a bronze bust of Hampton. I'm told it's very impressive. And now, at last, the book is back, reminding us that Hampton Hawes's contribution to jazz was twofold—as musician and memoirist.

GARY GIDDINS
May 1979

For Josie Black

Books by Don Asher

The Piano Sport

Don't the Moon Look Lonesome

The Electric Cotillion

The Eminent Yachtsman & The Whorehouse Piano Player

by Hampton Hawes and Don Asher

Raise Up Off Me

Raise Up Off Me

1

Flash Gordon of the Niggers

We used to call some of them jackleg preachers. Their robes rich as rubies in sunlight, preaching in their resonant voices, eyes checking the collection plates come in. And Mondays they'd be out juicing, seven card stud, low ball, balling anything they could lay their hands on. It was their trip, how they made their living, and I don't put them down for it. If folks were dumb enough to believe that jive, they can't rightfully complain.

But I've never seen so many people turned around, messed up, and disillusioned as I did when I was a kid going to church. My father wasn't one of the jacklegs. My brother and I called him "Sevener" 'cause when he went hunting in his sheepskin leggings and funny coat and hat he looked like someone out of 1847. He was a straight-ahead faith-dealing Presbyterian minister, a believer in the Three G's—Grits in your stomach, Grace in your heart, Greenbacks in your pocket (get all three down and you're cool)—and his people poured into his church on Sunday mornings like driving into a gas station to tank up with enough fuel to see them through the rest of the week. Get your ass kicked outside or come on in brothers and sisters, get

1

down on your knees and pray to God. "Mornin', Reverend Hawes." "Lovely sermon, Reverend Hawes." Ready to write testimonials to the good things that happened to them because of their faith. We see the light, Reverend, and the light is radiant, God is *it* (as if we didn't know) . . . "A beautiful mornin', Brother Brantley. How-d'ya-do, Sister Wells," and the kids mocking this adult form of address because, being affiliated with the church, it was automatically square. (How could we know that one day the people calling each other brother and sister would be Huey and Angela, Erica Huggins and Bobby Seale?) These same believing ladies in their starched white dresses whispering that my father mustn't be too holy, couldn't be a real righteous preacher or his wife wouldn't always have her belly so big. (*When you do it, do it for God. Meanwhile keep your pants up and your dresses down.*) They weren't bad people, just hurt and blind and scared, too scared to move past the middle of the bus, too scared to go to Gardena in 1935, seeing how quick the few rebellious ones got wasted. The church was their strength, the only thing they had where no one would mess with them. I never as a kid saw any outsider come in my old man's church and disturb anything. If them niggers is prayin', let 'em stay there; they're cool.

Our neighborhood at 35th and Budlong was a mixture of whites, blacks and Orientals with a few Mexicans around the edges. Negroes were niggers to both whites and themselves, and whites were peckerwood trash to Negroes and themselves. The Mexicans kept to themselves and ate tacos; the Negroes kept to themselves and ate collard greens. Both went to church out of fear and need, hoping the security and sophistication and sense of being part of the country would one day drift through the tall stained windows and warm them like the summer sun. The whites went to church for social and moral reasons; that's a big difference. But the minorities had one weapon, and that was language: If they wanted to turn you off, they just went into their native shit.

The Japanese mowed lawns and I don't know what else 'cause they were as mysterious to me as the Chinese who had laundries and grocery stores and sold dill pickles and big, fat glazed doughnuts to the black and Mexican kids. And the strange thing was, there was a peaceable mood in the country, a feeling of satisfaction and ease that people my age and older think of now as "the good old days." Ice cream parlors and the first Coke machines; Flash Gordon serials on Saturdays, jitterbugging to big bands; Bill Robinson and Shirley Temple (she was cute). A black musician who had a white woman and a Cadillac was a bad motherfucker. We identified with Errol Flynn, Ann Sheridan and Gloria De Haven; anybody who *looked* good was automatically a motherfucker. It holds to an extent today. Today Super Fly is the Flash Gordon of the niggers. Tells everyone to kiss his ass and wins, got all the bitches crumbling to him; plays a lone hand; big-time coke dealer, beats up on everyone who dares fight him. He's worse than Flash Gordon, he's the Lone Ranger. . . . The "good old days" when Franklin Roosevelt sat by a fire and talked to us through one of those funny little radios shaped like a birdhouse, when Stepinfetchit and Rochester were it, and the day after my father moved into the neighborhood at 35th and Budlong someone threw a rock through the window.

2

Come by My House

I was born with six fingers on each hand on November 13, 1928. The sixths were more like stubs than fingers and were snipped off with a nylon string on my third day of life at General Hospital in Los Angeles. But later, when I started picking out things on our parlor piano and what I played felt good, I wondered if it could have been some kind of omen.

I think I must have first turned to the piano out of boredom and loneliness. We were a reserved and undemonstrative family. The only time my mother kept me close was when she was at the piano and I'd put my hands on hers while she played; that was a kick, her hands moved so beautifully and it was like I was playing.

After a few early years of church I was left to myself on Sundays, puzzled at why those people in my father's church had to go through so many changes to do things that are supposed to be natural. All that kneelin' 'n shoutin'. Waving a cross to make a devil leave. Why not just beat him to death, tell him to get the fuck out of the way. If a kid gets up Sunday morning wanting to lay around, have a peanut butter sandwich with jelly and a pop first thing 'cause he's feeling good, or an adult has eyes for some wine or a Scotch, get himself all tore up, I thought Why not if that's the way he wants to go? No need to be ashamed of your feelings, ain't hurtin' nobody. I felt pulled apart watching so many people acting one way in the church and a different way in the street or in their backyards. Too many Dr. Jekylls in this show. Five days of the week I'm stuck at school with a raft of strange little kids forced to do this and that; after school things loosen up a bit—Kick the Can and the Flash Gordon serials on Saturday —then comes Sunday, wash off the grease, scrub your face, put on a coat and tie and a funny smile. What I liked to do best in school was draw: pictures of navy dudes in epaulets, airplanes and pilots in their air force suntans; 1 drew wagon wheel tracks narrowing in the distance while the other kids just drew parallel lines. I must have been pretty good at it 'cause the teacher called my mother and said your boy has a gift, got a way about him, ought to be in the movies. Wanting to put me in the movies when on certain days I couldn't even *go* to the movies. There were too many divisions, no flow between different days of the week; nothing matched up. Saturday I'm smiling because I'm happy and the next day you want me to change the clothes *and* the smile. Why not let me keep the smile and go greasy and tieless 'cause that's my natural state, and you shouldn't be afraid of meeting the Maker and paying your respects in that state. Motherfucker just might *expect* it. It seemed like the transitions were too rough, like a spliced film jumping in the projector. Whoever was in charge of the show was playing games, trying to confuse us.

When I was six I was given a little gold Sunday school pin which was the reward you got for a year's good attendance. But three years later I had stopped going to church Sundays and was listening to Freddie Slack, Fats Waller (bad cats) and Earl Hines (very bad cat) playing his "Boogie-Woogie on St. Louis Blues," using the time the family was at church to pick out some of that stuff on our parlor piano.

The piano was the only sure friend I had because it was the only thing that was consistent, always made sense and responded directly to what I did. Pianos don't ever change. Sittin' there every day. You wanna play me, here I am. The D is still here, the A flat's still here, they're always going to be there and it don't matter whether it's Sunday, Ash Wednesday or the Fourth of July. Play it right and it comes out right; mess with it and it'll make you back up. A piano don't lie. Check the prancing players with the sparkles in their eyes and the pretty fingernails flashing up and down the keyboard—listen closely and that's all there is, just flash and icing, no more depth or meaning than a wood chip dancing down a waterfall. A keyboard is more consistent than life, it gives you back what you put into it, no more, no less. In the forties Bud Powell had grease in his veins and burned the motherfucker up; Thelonious Monk plays it strange and beautiful because he *feels* strange and beautiful. The piano was the first secure and honest thing in my life, I could approach it on my own and fail or be good. Straight to the point and quick.

It didn't take me long to reason that if Sunday's too holy for boogie-woogie and Flash Gordon movies, if Sunday's messed up for good things like that, then Saturday is too, and Wednesday; shouldn't be any one day for it. Don't tell me I can go out in the street and kick a dog on Wednesday, but on Sunday it wouldn't be cool. Didn't sound right. So one day I told him, Sevener, if it's a sin on Sunday, it's a sin any day. Fuck Sunday. If you can't be righteous and believe what you want and do what you want every day then something's wrong. Whoever wrote the rules—probably the same dudes in the Sunday school books who sat up in the stands eating grapes and throwing people to the lions—messed up. I began seriously questioning the other ordained rules too, meanwhile collecting my records and picking things off them to play.

My mother backed me up—she'd had it long ago with the bitches in their starched whites staring at her belly, thinking, Reverend's uncool, sinful, oughta be above that sort of thing— and said that seeing how I felt, she wouldn't insist on raising me in the church. Sevener was a gentle man and understanding, but his faith was strong as oak and he couldn't countenance boogie on Sunday. One of my sisters, thinking she was helping him combat sin and thereby hold off the Lord's wrath, took to locking the piano Sundays when the family set out for church. I finally found the place she'd hid the key so as soon as they took off I'd unlock, play my stuff, and when it was time for them to come home, lock it back up, pick up my Batman or Terry and the Pirates comics with the Ann Sheridan glossies stuck inside and be sitting there cool when they walked in.

Now it must sound strange that a black preacher wouldn't let his own kid play the inbred music of the times, so to speak. But in the environs of 35th and Budlong the heroes of the Negro community were George Washington Carver and Rochester. Fats and Louis and Earl Hines were looked down on, were a source of pride only to the street people, pimps, and nightclub habitués. Those cats played in clubs where booze was served to gangsters and other people of ill repute, and chicks in groovy dresses smoked cigarettes. All that was considered heavy sin, but it sounded like fun to me and made a lot more sense than kneelin' down on a hardwood floor in a starched white shirt sayin' Hallelujah all the goddamn day. I dug the piano so much, I figured the other part of the scene must be cool too. But I didn't think at the time that I might have a talent or gift, it was just the freedom and the music drawing me.

My sister Mabel played piano too. She was studying to be a concert pianist and when she'd finish practicing I'd head straight to the upright and try to pick up on her shit. Sevener never hid the key from her. She played Rachmaninoff's C Minor Concerto for a Gold's Furniture Store contest and won first prize, one of those funny birdhouse radios.

The important thing is, a lot of the best black musicians had family in the ministry. Charlie Parker's uncle was Bishop Peter E. Parker and Nat Cole's father was a minister. Dig it. When I was in my teens and started hanging out and jamming with those cats they'd say, Come by my house. And when I came by their houses and met their mothers and sisters, their mothers and sisters would remind me of people I used to see in my father's church on Sunday. So we were the first generation to rebel, playing bebop, trying to be different, going through a lot of changes and getting strung out in the process. *What those crazy niggers doin' playin' that crazy music?* Wild. Out of the jungle. But so long as they're not lootin' no stores or shootin' our asses, leave 'em be.

Though we were rebelling, we were doing it musically, nonviolently, and most people didn't know what was coming down. Now there's another generation of rebels and these kids are doing things we wouldn't have dared because we knew we wouldn't have got away with it and were smart enough not to try. Our rebellion was a form of survival. If we didn't do that what else could we do? Get your hair gassed, brothers, put on your bow ties and a funny smile and play pretty for the rich white folks. We were pilgrims, the freaks of the forties and fifties; our rebellion was a lonely thing. The kids rebelling with their music today got a whole Woodstock nation behind them.

When I started playing professionally and recording, my family hardly ever came to hear me play—my sisters once in a great while, but never my father or brother—they still didn't understand where I was coming from. But what they'd do is this: When I sent them one of my albums, if the jacket made a pretty picture (never mind if it bore a good *likeness* of me), why they'd put it in a frame and hang it up on the wall.

My brother Wesley loved and admired Sevener and followed him into the ministry. Graduated the seminary and for six years preached at a funny little storefront church in San Francisco. Tired of it and went to New York where he got a job with the department of recreation and parks. Today he's nervous and beautiful. When I was last East I went to visit him at his house on Long Island; brought him a tie as a present. The next morning I looked out the window and saw him mowing the lawn wearing a T-shirt and the tie. I said, "What you doin' with the tie on?" He said, "You gave me the tie, didn't you?" I said, "Sure." He said, "You know when you was four years old you used to call me a fool." I said, "Well if I called you that maybe you was. You like the tie?" "It's OK," he said.

The memories sometimes lie like thick soup sitting a long while and you have to stir up what's on the bottom. I'm remembering Brother Brantley, a heavy member of the congregation, a deacon in fact, showing up like clockwork every Sunday in his little black tie . . . *Morning, Reverend . . . A*

good morning to you, Sister . . . and after the sermon, *You
told it fine, Reverend, you absolutely right on that score.* My
father would ask him to come by the house and offer him coffee and doughnuts. Now dig his game. He'd finish his coffee
and have half a doughnut left and say, I'd sure like another
coffee to go with this fine doughnut. Then he'd finish the
doughnut and say, This coffee sure is fine, wish I had another
doughnut to go with it. And the dude would stay there right
through the morning, eating doughnuts and coffee. And next
Sunday be the first to testify, *God's right. Put the cross up,
Reverend* . . . After I started playing jazz and getting wild,
Dexter Gordon and I one night brought two chicks back to
the pad. They were so happy they kept climbing the stairs and
sliding down the banister naked; run up and slide back down
again and not even the sound of the doorbell stopped them.
It was Brother Brantley looking for my father who was at the
hospital because my sister Gertrude was dying. Which shows
you where my mind was at that time, balling chicks in my
own house and my sister dying. Brother Brantley stood on the
threshold and his eyes lit up. Watching those joyful young
chicks sliding down the banister. Wanted to come in, wished
he would've said so. But he was a deacon in my father's
church. At last he tore his eyes away from the naked bodies
and said, "You know what, Hampton? You OK."

You keep looking back. The years when it seemed like
every day was Sunday, Reverend Hawes this and Reverend
Hawes that, broads in their stiff white dresses jumpin' up and
down, "We see the light, Reverend, and the light is radiant!"
(*Shun the weed, keep idle hands out of your pockets.*) "Tell
it all, Reverend!" (*Don't lift the little girls' dresses.*) "Care to
drop by for some chicken, Reverend Hawes?" . . . And you

know, all those years I would've given anything to hear someone say, no airs or pomp or formality, just, "Hello, Mr.
Hawes," or "Hey, man." It would have been refreshing.

He's in his early eighties now, retired ten years. Still lives in
the house at 35th and Budlong with one of my sister's daughters. Once in a while he'll put on his robe and officiate at a
funeral because someone in their will has asked for him. A
little while ago a friend of mine who'd been on the road for
years stopped me on the street in Berkeley where I was recording a new album. He'd been to a funeral in L.A. the day before
and said, "Hey, Hamp, I didn't know your old man was still
gigging."

He had God in his heart and understood, and I didn't. At
six I thought he was a spokesman for God, passing the word
down that Sundays were sacred and fucked up for humans.
But I didn't meet God, or a facsimile of him, till years later
at the Hi-De-Ho Club at 50th and Western, playing alto in the
Howard McGhee band.

3

At the Hi-De-Ho

One of the great tracks in jazz is Charlie Parker's "Parker's Mood." It begins with a three-note figure contained in a G minor triad—in this sequence: Bb-G-D—and whenever you heard someone whistling those notes in L.A., you knew you were in the presence of a friend. It signified you were using but cool, and when you went to buy dope late at night (which was the usual time to cop) if the bell wasn't working or you didn't want to jar the Man out of a sound sleep or there might be someone uncool on the premises, you went *Bb-G-D* in that fast, secret way and the cat would pop his head out the window. When Bird first played his "Parker's Mood" I think those notes might have been drifting around somewhere in his head and they just flew right out.

In 1947 I graduated from Polytechnic High School, split out the back of the auditorium (thinking, *Damn, I'm free, got my diploma and didn't fuck up, can sleep till twelve tomorrow*), threw my cap and gown in the back of the Ford and made it only fifteen minutes late to The Last Word where I was working with the Jay McNeely band. A few months later I joined Howard McGhee's Quintet at the Hi-De-Ho. Bird had

12

worked his way back from the East Coast and joined us. When I had first heard him at Billy Berg's in 1945 I couldn't believe what he was doing, how anyone could so totally block out everything extraneous, light a fire that hot inside him and constantly feed on that fire. Now at the time there were maybe ten people in the neighborhood of 50th and Western who knew there was a genius playing alto. Most people who had heard him thought he was crazy. His playing was too free and blazing and pure; it could be dissonant and harsh on the ears if you weren't accustomed to the sound. He had already recorded those early classics with Dizzy but you couldn't find the records on any jukeboxes. Today the DJ's can take a new sound and spread it like flash fire; before you know it you're on television beaming to thirty million people. But this was before TV, and jazz was years away from reaching the concert halls. The only people in the vicinity of 50th and Western who were hip to him were a few of the street people, one or two chicks at the house where he was staying—the woman who owned it, a madame with a whorehouse on the east side, was a good friend of his and put him up whenever he was in town—and, of course, other musicians. When word got around where he was playing they came to check him out. Motherfuckers peeked and backed right up. Those of us who were affected the strongest felt we'd be willing to do anything to warm ourselves by that fire, get some of that grease pumping through our veins. He fucked up all our minds. It was where the ultimate truth was.

As with anyone that heavy and different, some people were awed or afraid of him and kept their distance. Others pursued him, would drop by his pad and hang out, figuring if they were around him long enough some of his shit was bound to rub off on them. I watched motherfuckers write down his solos note for note, play them on their own gigs and then wonder why they didn't sound as good. And if they had to follow Bird's solo with their own stuff, that would really leave them exposed —like standing naked and wet in a cold wind. Bird would take advantage of these dudes, borrow money and burn them in various ways. It wasn't that he was a bad cat, any junkie would do the same thing. It was a matter of dope or no dope; survival. Bird was out and he was strung, and in order to be around him you had to contend with that.

I never crowded or bothered him. I was busy trying to figure out my own life and I sensed that aside from his music it wasn't going to do me any good to be spending a lot of time around Bird. But he was the best player in the game, and on the stand when he'd sometimes look around at me and smile I knew I had played something good.

He was a sad driver—when his two-year-old car fell apart he left it in the street; borrowed mine once and tried to shift without using the clutch—so I'd pick him up every night at the madame's house in my '37 Ford, take him to work and bring him back. When I came early one night he motioned me to follow him to his room. I waded through piles of sandwich wrappers, beer cans and liquor bottles. Watched him line up and take down eleven shots of whiskey, pop a handful of bennies, then tie up, smoking a joint at the same time. He sweated like a horse for five minutes, got up, put on his suit and a half hour later was on the stand playing strong and beautiful.

For two weeks he never said a word to me—going to the club, on the stand, or driving home. But it wasn't an uncomfortable silence; he was either stoned, froze, or just off somewhere else, and I respected whatever trip he was on and whatever distant place it carried him to. It was never an ego trip. If someone were to ask him who he liked better on alto, Henry Prior or Sonny Criss—it was the sort of thing a young player starting to come up would ask—he'd shrug and say, Both. They're both cool. Shooting down other players was as foreign to his nature as a longing for sharp clothes and a Cadillac or whether or not he had a white woman, which were the black badges of success in those days. He had plenty of white women but it never interfered with his music.

Sometimes I'd pull up in front of the club and he'd be too high to get out of the car. Howard McGhee would ask me where Bird was. I'd say, Sittin' in the car. No point in trying to pull him out, he wouldn't have been able to play anyway. After a while he'd get himself together, walk in and start blowing—even before he reached the stand, weaving his way through the tables playing in that beautiful, fiery way.

At the end of the second week of the gig he spoke his first words to me. It was close to three in the morning when I left him off at the madame's house. He got out, started walking toward the house, then stuck his head back in the window and said, "I heard you tonight."

The next day I told the guys in the band I was going to drop by Bird's place and see if he wanted to go to a movie. Everybody said, That's a dumb idea, he isn't going to want to go to any show. That's too square for him, too bourgeois. I dropped by anyway. He came to the door in a T-shirt and the same pin-stripe suit he wore on the stand. Said it was a nice day and a show sounded like a good idea. We went to a newsreel playing nearby. As I was buying my ticket I realized Bird was no longer with me. Looked up and down the street and saw him coming out of an alley halfway down the block. He wandered up to the box office and laid out his money, not saying anything about the little side trip. Afterwards we ate a hot dog and dróve around downtown in my Ford, enjoying the spring day. When I dropped him off back at the house he said, "I had a nice time."

That weekend I smoked my first joint, some light green from Chicago Bird pulled out as we were driving down Avalon Boulevard to get a hamburger and Coke. Didn't feel anything till after we ate and I started driving home. I said, Man, why are all these horns honking at me? Bird said, You're driving backwards. I stopped and let him take over the wheel. He made it back to his place, stripping gears all the way. I walked the ten blocks to my house and was weaving up to the door when I saw a tiny old lady from my father's church staring at me. Watched me trying to make it to the door and said, "Young man, are you behaving yourself?" I made it up the stairs, lay down under the bed, and getting a flash from the old church days asked God aloud to deliver me from the devil.

Next day Bird phoned me and said, "That was some powerful light green."

His uncle was Bishop Peter E. Parker and maybe he was close to God. I know he was damn near like a prophet in his music. He scared a lot of people over the years and died of pneumonia, so they say, in Baroness Nica Rothschild's Fifth Avenue living room when he was thirty-four. But as long as I knew Bird, I was never awed or afraid of him. I loved him. And how can you be afraid of somebody you love?

4

University of the Streets
of New York

I've been shot at and missed and shit at and hit. That's a saying out of my childhood and it's come true more than a few times along the way.

During the year or two following high school I wasn't yet thinking about a career. My main interests were in buying me a car, put some twin pipes and a skirt on it, get a new shirt, go to a show, find a girl. I didn't know Sylvia was a prostitute until the day she bought me a fine suede coat after we'd been together about two weeks. When I asked her where she got her bread (since she spent so much time at home), she said, I make it turning tricks with middle-aged businessmen with beady eyes. She'd run down for me daily accounts of the various tricks—the gangster who always put his hat back on before the rest of his clothes, a Catholic priest who made her dress in a pinafore and saddle shoes. I wondered what those cats would have thought if they had known that this fine dark-haired bitch for which they were putting out $75–$100 was coming home every night to a teen-age nigger.

17

At the other end of the wage scale I was making $10–$15 a night playing with some heavy cats, but because I was under twenty-one my father had to cosign for almost everything: union membership, driver's license, bank account. Here I was making good bread for that time, buying my own clothes, even paying my mother to iron my shirts, putting the rest in the bank (who else at age nineteen had almost $2,000 in the bank in 1948?), thrifty, together, responsible, taking care of business, and every time I wanted to do something decisive I had to get a cosignature. I was a man and felt like a kid. Sevener wouldn't cosign for a 1947 Buick I wanted, thought there was something suspicious about a year-old Buick for only seven bills, and the fact that his suspicions were correct—Sylvia, who was going to split the cost with me was tricking the local used-car dealer Honest Abe (who would wind up in San Quentin two years later)—the fact that Sevener smelled something funny in the deal didn't make me feel any better. A wage-earning money-saving tax-paying citizen (respectful, sober and acting older than his years), and the law wouldn't allow me to make decisions or control my own future; refused me my identity. The same law that later dragged me and Sylvia out of our Buick at Hermosa Beach, wanting to know if she was there of her own free will and if her mother knew she was out with a nigger. Playing righteous music in all those funky bars and I wasn't even supposed to *drink* in one. I was Hampton B. Hawes, *Jr.*, and I've always resented the "Jr." Eighty-nine years old, you still sound like a little kid playing at being an adult (like I did when I was five, thinking I was a giant eating trees when I ate my broccoli, and watching my brother and sisters go off to school, then taking a jelly sandwich in a paper bag and a bunch of books I couldn't read into the garage and making believe I was out there with them). And that's some cold shit.

Funny things began happening with Sylvia. She'd say she was going to pick me up at my father's house at nine and wouldn't show till two. Tell me she was sick or had her period, lock herself in the bathroom (I was so ignorant and naive in those years I thought she had a bladder problem) and an hour later be feeling okay. When I finally learned she was strung we had drifted apart. She gave me back part of my bread and split with the Buick. A year later I heard she was doing time in Tehachapi.

Word had filtered to our coast that things were happening in New York. With nothing to keep me in L.A. for the moment I bought a ticket on a nonscheduled airline. Never been on a plane before and got a little nervous when I learned that the cat selling tickets was the copilot, then a few minutes later saw the *pilot* paying the gas-truck man out of his own pocket. The stewardess was wearing ski pants and a fur coat with one of those animal-head collars. Handed me a khaki blanket as I came on board and said, "Bundle up tight, honey, it's gonna be a long cold trip."

Wardell Gray, a saxophone player and friend from L.A., who was working with Benny Goodman at the Paramount Theater, fixed me up with a room on 116th Street, a few blocks from Central Park. The landlady looked like she was a couple of notches past sixty, dumpy and flat-footed, wore a bandanna; when I saw Moms Mabley some years later I thought for a minute it must be the same woman. The landlady had a little cup in the kitchen where you left a dime if you wanted coffee. The second night she knocked on my door and told me she could get me a girl but if it was urgent she could handle it herself. "Don't let these wrinkles fool you, I still got some miles left." Next day I found out she sold dope and hot clothes on the side. I had to admire her spirit.

Wardell took me to Minton's, the Royal Roost and Small's Paradise where the players who had triggered the rebellion and put fire in the music were burning those clubs up. It was intense but beautiful music and I began to see why a lot of them had to stay stoned to play it. Made me wonder what Stravinsky went through with *The Rite of Spring*. Technically and emotionally what Bird and Bud Powell and the others were doing must have been just as difficult—maybe more so, because it was extemporaneous—and in order to play it every night they had to adjust to so many inner changes, blow their minds so far out to encompass the quick-shifting harmonies and note-patterns and at the same time block the hostility from critics and fellow musicians (Louis Armstrong, one of the original brothers, complaining, *Them cats play all the wrong notes*), and all the shit going on out front of the stage (*crazy niggers playin' that wild music*)—that there was a tremendous drive to turn inward, stay blind, blot it all out.

One night at Minton's, a club in Harlem where there were all-night sessions, somebody recognized me and said, "There's a cat from California supposed to play good, let's get him up here." Now at that time there were a lot of East Coast musicians who thought it slick to try to shoot down anyone new on the scene who was starting to make a reputation. It was like an initiation, a ceremonial rite (*chump, jump or I'll burn you up, you don't know nothin'*), calling far-out tunes in strange keys with the hip changes at tempos so fast if you didn't fly you fell—that's how you earned your diploma in the University of the Streets of New York.

For a week I had watched these cats burning each other up, ambushing outsiders, fucking up their minds so bad they would fold and split the stand after one tune. Surprised by their coldness because they were so friendly off the stand. I peeked that I wasn't quite ready, maybe they could get me; you don't want to be a poopbutt but sometimes it's better to pass, wait for a better hand. I knew I wouldn't flop, but neither would I win acclaim. No point in selling tickets if you don't have a show.

The challenge lifted me a few notches—I knew I had to go out and tighten my hand—and when I came back that way a couple of years later, strung out, five albums under my belt and a lot of playing with Bird, I was ready for them; they couldn't make me feel funny anymore and left me alone after that. A drummer paid me the ultimate compliment following a set: "We been hearin' about you out on the coast, you a bad motherfucker." My days of being scared and nervous—at least about music—were over.

It's too bad it had to be that way, cutting friends up to make them feel inferior so they could get better. That isn't what music is about. You play for love and for people to enjoy. It's okay to show a few feathers, you got to have pride in yourself, but you shouldn't have to wear boxing gloves and spurs; this ain't no cockfight or main bout at Madison Square Garden. We're all brothers, aren't we?—came up the same way, earned our diplomas listening, picking up, hanging out, nervous, some of us getting busted? Yet when I think back, the system did serve a purpose. Blacks in those days had to bear down hard to handle the shadow that was always haunting them, and the constant challenge was the pressure cooker in which you earned recognition and respect. In the process the music grew leaner, tightened up; the ones who didn't have it, who couldn't contribute, fell away. If you don't have credentials, stay off of Fifth Avenue.

Today when I go to New York the young musicians who never heard me play because I was out of circulation for a while, maybe never even heard my records—aren't even sure if I can *play* anymore—they know about me. They have heard I was through here before and earned my credits at the University.

After two weeks in New York, my money giving out, I connected with Wild Bill Moore's traveling band. He was a saxophone player I'd known from L.A.; played a high squeaky horn, sounded like a vampire bat in heat, which was why they called him Wild Bill. We worked our way down the coast, through Philly and Washington, D.C., to North Carolina. It was my first trip South. In Washington we played for Howard University at Turner's Arena, which was a boxing club. I thought it was stupid for a band to play in a boxing club, but they took the ring down and had themselves a good dance. When all those bitches in their long gowns piled into the place it opened my nose. I'd never seen so many sophisticated-looking black chicks in one place at one time, and I remembered Sevener telling me about Howard; he'd gone to Lincoln, and Howard and Lincoln were rivals, he said, like Harvard and Yale. I thought if I had one of them fine bitches back in L.A., I'd put on my best shirt and take her down to Central and 42nd, let all the people dig her.

On the ferryboat crossing Chesapeake Bay I was heading

into the bathroom when the drummer, an older cat, grabbed my arm, turned me around and pointed me toward a sign in the far corner that said COLORED. Never seen one of those before. And an hour later when it was time for lunch we were told to go to the rear deck where there was an outside counter serving chiliburgers and pop. Had to eat standing up, spray whipping our faces, while looking into a big glass-enclosed room: white people spreading napkins in their laps, two different kinds of forks beside the plates and a little bowl of flowers on each table. I turned to the drummer and said, Man, there's some funny kind of shit going on down here.

In North Carolina we played a concert in an armory and I got my first look at mass segregation. The white folks were all in the upstairs gallery and the blacks on the ground floor. We stayed in a boarding house, three beds to a room, where another Moms Mabley stand-in charged us a quarter for an extra blanket (I never knew it got so cold in the South) and fifty cents to take a shower. Wanted to press our clothes and cook for us too, but we told her we weren't aiming to leave the Southland broke.

Wild Bill had a few more gigs which would have taken us back up to New York, but I was starting to see a long string of arenas and armories and chicken-shack boarding houses stretching out before me and I knew I didn't want to live my life that aimlessly. At the same time the idea was building in my head that I could go a fairly long ways in music. I had played with the heaviest cats in California and sat in at some of the New York clubs, and from what I had heard of the other piano players on the East Coast scene I knew I was at least in the same league. The Wild Bill Moore trip had been good experience, I had dug working with those guys, but the caliber of the music just wasn't the same as that going on in the Manhattan clubs. That fiery, rebellious but beautiful sound was drawing me and I knew there was no more to learn on the road; I wasn't going to become no jazz immortal playing with Wild Bill. Then too, I was getting homesick. I had just turned nineteen. On a cold, rainy afternoon in Raleigh just before Christmas, lonely, nothing else to do, I went to a movie, *The Snake Pit*. It was a straight-ahead and honest film, but depressing, pair of old ladies in fur coats sniffling in the row behind me, and at the end when the voices came on the sound track singing, "Going home, going home . . ." in that tearful but hopeful way, it worked on me like a bell ringing for a caged animal. My heart turned over a little and I knew it was time I was getting back to that other, sunnier coast.

5

Lady

Red Norvo offered me a job at Cafe Society in San Francisco. I couldn't read chords too well at the time and had to rely on my ear. Whenever I played a wrong chord, Red—he had a big pot belly then—would turn round, bug his eyes, wave his mallets at me and go *"Accchhh!"* I hated that bogeyman stuff, but it's partly the reason I hear so good today.

Billie Holiday was working opposite us, sounding so good, like her heart was breaking on every tune. She was a rowdy, soulful, bighearted woman; carried around a pair of those little dogs you put sweaters on. At that time she was already famous and narcotics agents were harassing her. She got so she could spot them at fifty feet through a haze of smoke. "See the little cat drinking Manhattans in the brown suit? Po-lice," she'd say.

She could be tender and show a temper that would scorch you. "I'm gonna come down off this stand and kick your ass," she said to a chick who had been talking non-stop through her opening-night show; and afterwards told the bass player, who liked to stretch out behind singers, "Why you have to play so wild? Cut out that devil music." That cat took it so to heart he just looked at her quietly and his eyes filled with tears.

Later that night some of the musicians were arguing in the band room when she hollered from her dressing room—banging on the wall separating the two—"Shut up all that noise in there." They yelled back, "Shut up yourself, broad" . . . "Come in and make us." We heard her door slam and a second later she came barging into our room in her draws. She was big and strong, had some righteous meat on her, and those cats flattened against the wall, grinning, their arms raised. I watched it all from my chair in the corner. She glared a minute, then walked back out, talkin' about crazy motherfuckers, and said to me, "You don't need to flinch, baby, I know it wasn't you."

From that night on she began coming by the piano after her show when I would play intermission music. Would lean over me and say stuff like, "You're about the sweetest quietest cat I ever seen, you play so pretty. Takin' care of business and not chasin' the scroungy ass bitches that come in here . . ." She was always having trouble with men—when she went for someone it was wholehearted, she'd really mix it up with him and he usually had the bag*—but I was barely twenty, never jived or bothered her, and maybe that was why she liked to come over and talk. She made it her business to see that the chicks who hung out in the club didn't hit on me. "You leave him alone, he's nice, keep your funky hands off him." I had the feeling she hoped I wouldn't have to go through any bad changes, almost like a mother anxious for her son to steer clear of booze and drugs and sin; didn't want anyone polluting me. I didn't realize at the time that there was no way of escaping all that, I'd eventually have to go through it; you got to wade through a certain amount of mud to get to the pearls.

---

* Narcotics and works.

We were leaving the club together one night when some photographers started taking pictures of her. "If you're gonna snap me," she said, "you gotta include my son," and she pulled me over, hugging and squeezing me. It was a hoked-up but nice picture and I still have it hanging over my mantel in East L.A.

One afternoon toward the end of the gig some agents broke down the door of her hotel room looking for dope. If they'd come an hour earlier or an hour or so later she could've handled it, but at the time they broke in she and her man had their clothes off. They searched the room and busted her, but a good criminal lawyer up there, Jake Erlich, got her off. It was only temporary relief though. They kept hounding her till the end of her days, and despite what the obituaries and the movie said, I know she died because she was too emotional and bighearted, always racing. She lived her life so full it was inevitable she would go down fast.

6

Seventeen Green Buicks

You come out of the haven of the church humble and unsure, turning the other cheek, trying to find some balance in your life and life slapping you down every day—you either cave or you get mad. I didn't do either; I went through center, thought I'd make a touchdown. I reasoned, if I can't get anywhere playing by the rules, let's turn things around, see what the other end looks like; can't be much worse, might be a shade better. Balance tips funny to one side, weigh it down on the other; take your destiny out of other people's hands; fucked up on land, jump in the sea. But *try something different*. And that something different was what a lot of cats were into and they all seemed to be grooving—confident, sophisticated, independent, not hurting or not much anyway, hostility slipping away, new lease on life . . . What is this shit? . . . Now at a young and impressionable age you're standing on the curb and see seventeen cats swing by in seventeen green Buicks, wouldn't you start to wonder, What's with the green Buick?

The Central Avenue clubs had caught fire and were jumping into the sunrise. Alabam, Downbeat, The Last Word,

28

Jungle Room, and the after-hours spots which had setups out front, bottles for sale in the back room. Our music was catching on, drawing the pimps and prostitutes, dealers, promotors, pool-hall players, and the white middle-class chicks, the rebels who were turning away from secretary gigs and Horace Heidt, pulled by the realness of the black music and the excitement and hipness of the atmosphere. They were our biggest fans, looked down on as sluts in their own communities, but they didn't give a shit; like the hippies of the sixties they were cultural pioneers, drawn by something genuine, the main difference being that in those days they dressed like everyone else, so externally you couldn't distinguish a Horace Heidt follower from a Charlie Parker fan. The musicians never looked down on them and treated them right, though an occasional brother on a power trip might use and exploit them. (*"If you wanna dwell in my sunshine, pick up my shit."*)

Now there was nothing that would shake the L.A. cops more than the sight of people of different races together. On any weekend night on Central Avenue in the forties you could probably see more blinking red lights than on any other thoroughfare in the country. Seen from a distance you'd think it was some kind of far-out holocaust, a fifty-car smashup, Watts '65. But it was only the cops jamming* brothers—the same cops who'd come into the after-hours clubs for their cut—making them roll up their sleeves, patting 'em down. *Turn out your pockets, we got a tip there's dope in this car.* It wasn't unusual for a whole club of mixed couples to be paraded down to the Newton Street station for a mass inspection and pat-down. The night Billy Eckstine came by Jack's Basket Room to hear me and Wardell Gray play, he wasn't

---

* Harassing.

with a white woman, but he was in possession of something equally suspicious: a new Cadillac with out-of-state plates. They opened the trunk to make a search. He tried to explain the New York plates by showing them identification, but they still took him away and B. wasn't able to make it down to Central Avenue until several hours later. Those were dangerous years; it had to be dedication and love of the music that kept those people coming on the scene, subjecting themselves to that kind of abuse.

The pimp-dealers were drawn to the scene by something more than the music: a steady clientele for their dope and access to the fine chicks who hung around the musicians. It was a San Francisco pimp who first turned me on. He's respectable now, owns a string of taco places and an office building, sends his daughter to Mills, so I'll call him by a phony name, John Dandy. A couple of us were talking to John Dandy after work one night and he was telling us, "I don't understand you guys, you draw all the chicks, but when you get them you don't know what to do with them." Wardell said, "We're playing music, we ain't interested in pimping. So if you want to pimp, you pimp, but don't bother us about how we treat chicks." John Dandy said, "You're too nice to them is all I'm saying," and someone else told him, "They're our fans, man, what else we going to do but be nice to 'em?"

After a while the others drifted off and John Dandy invited me over to his house. We got comfortable and he said, You want to snort some of this? At the time I was smoking a little pot, but most everyone else seemed to be on the other trip so I said, OK. Might as well jump in, see how cool the water is. Then to put the icing on, he called in one of his bitches and told her to go home with me and make me even more comfortable than I was. We went back to the room where I was staying, I lay down on the bed, drowsy and happy, and watched her get ready to take her clothes off. I said, Don't do that, just sit on the side and hold my hand. Limp and loose, with this fine bitch holding my hand, I began nodding, drifting off. I'd never felt like that before, unconcerned and complete, no strain and no wants. I didn't need her in bed with me; with just the tiniest jump of imagination my whole body was a dick and into something fine, so all I had to do really was just stay happy and groove.

Everybody I knew, except Wardell, was using heroin at that time. Some were turned on by Bird—not by him directly, but reasoning that if they went out and got fucked up like him they might get closer to the source of his fire. Some learned, and others never did, that junk has no more to do with playing good than the make of your short* or the shade of your skin. I knew a lot of strung-out dudes who couldn't play shit; they should have just got high and enjoyed themselves and forgot about playing. If you can't swing, you can't swing. You can stuff your stomach with black-eyed peas and chitlins, go out and roll in the mud and say I'm gonna get down,** but it ain't going to help if you don't pat your feet right because chitlins have no more to do with soul than mud has to do with music. If you say to Little Lord Fauntleroy, Go roll three times over there in that shit, get good and funky, then come back and play the same tune, see if it helps, you know what would happen? He'd roll over three times, come back and play the same tune, and the only difference would be that he'd be covered

---

* Car.
** Soulful.

with shit. Music's the same as life, there ain't no corners, no outs. It was the times and the environment that strung most of us out. You're on the way to the gig, you see some cats tying up, you think, All right, let me try some of that; like a kid riding his first bicycle, drinking his first cherry pop. You try it, it feels good, and there you go. And the casualty list in the fifties—dead, wounded, and mentally deranged—started to look like the Korean War was being fought at the corner of Central and 45th.

7

Keepers of the Flame

Of the regular players along Central Avenue, Wardell Gray, Dexter Gordon and Teddy Edwards (and Bird when he was in town) were the keepers of the flame, the ones the younger players held in esteem for their ideas and experience and consistency. Wardell was like a big brother to me. When I had gone to New York at eighteen and sat in at the Royal Roost, played a couple choruses of "How High the Moon" that brought the pianist back in a hurry, it was Wardell who took me aside and said, "I'm proud of you." He carried books by Sartre with him and talked about Henry Wallace and the NAACP. When white fans in the clubs came up to speak to us, Wardell would do the talking while the rest of us clammed up and looked funny. He ate like a horse and was skinny as a nail. First time I saw him in his draws, ribs showing like a starving alley cat, I thought if I blew at him he'd fall over. Scared me. He couldn't have weighed a hundred pounds. I used to think of myself as Wardell's understudy or lieutenant. Aside from Bird he was the player we looked up to most, one of the few of the older, experienced cats who wasn't strung, and when he'd now and then counsel those of us who were starting to fuck with dope to get ourselves together and straighten up, we may not have accepted the advice, but neither did we resent it.

I was listening and growing. I had learned from Bird how to stay loose and relaxed on up tempos, and found out that at very slow tempos the beat has to swell: It's like taking a mouthful of good wine, swishing it around, savoring it before you let it go down; the swallow is that beat finally dropping.

By 1950 I was recording and beginning to appear in the jazz polls, but I haven't had much faith in polls since Jimmy Garrison told me how he had been stopped for speeding on the New York State Thruway. His wife got indignant and said to the cop, "You can't give him a ticket, he's the fifth best bass player in the United States." And the cop answered, "Lady, the only difference from now on is he's going to be the fifth best bass player in the United States with a moving violation."

In Las Vegas with Happy Johnson's band I found out that accommodations for black musicians were about on a par with North Carolina and the Chesapeake Bay ferryboat. We stayed in a shack across the tracks and had to sit out our intermissions in a little anteroom with folding chairs such as you see in a small-town doctor's office. One of the waitresses felt sorry for us and would drop in periodically to see if we wanted anything from the bar. Happy was an old cat out of the old school—might have gone all the way back to Louis Armstrong's time—and kept cautioning the younger players in the group to be cool, don't do that or go in there, they might not like it; the money's good so behave yourselves, don't go acting crazy or stirring things up. He couldn't help himself. He was a nice cat but a scared nigger, and one night when the sheriff came up to the bandstand and asked him if the band could dance, Happy's eyes got big as cartwheels and he started doing a little shuffle for the sheriff, an Uncle Remus-Br'er Rabbit step or two. Next night the sheriff came in again and Happy broke into his little steps before even being asked; sheriff laughed and clapped and that nigger's feet kept moving. That did it for me, I couldn't handle it anymore. I gave notice with one of the other young players and told Happy, You can tom as much as you want, but don't expect me to sit around and watch. The whole time I was there—cured for good of any desire to voluntarily see a desert again (though a little over a year later I'd be inhabiting an army stockade 120 miles west, penned in like a donkey in a corral under a sun as hot and inhuman as a branding iron)—the entire two weeks I saw only one black come into the club bar unmolested and that was Dorothy Donnegan, who was playing boogie-woogie piano at the Riviera, one of the big hotels on the Strip. Walked in one night with an ofay cat, dressed in one of those little cowboy outfits you see chicks wearing between halves on the football field, short, fringed skirt and vest, a string tie and leather boots.

Back home I left Sevener's house, got a room for $11 a week on 21st Street and joined the Jack McVea band on a trip that took us up through San Francisco to Seattle. (There was a fine drummer with the band, Chuck Thompson, who I would later team up with when I formed my first trio; his time was natural as a heartbeat pumping pure, fresh blood into a tune, his rolls so even it was like hearing a crowd roar during a big play at a football game on the radio with the volume turned down.) Jack had made a big hit with his recording of "Open the Door, Richard" and we had to play that sad-ass tune a couple of times every night, though in all fairness there would have been fewer gigs without it. Ray Charles' group played our intermissions in Seattle; he called himself something else then and was singing like Nat Cole. On the way out of town our girl singer fell out breathing half-and-half (oxygen-carbon monoxide) while trying to get some sleep in the back of the bus. We revived her with artificial respiration in a field, then crossed the road after our hard work to a little grocery and bought some Cokes which the proprietor made us take outside and drink in the road. In Lake Tahoe we found the gig we had lined up had been canceled. Back in San Francisco tragedy struck. Frank Clarke, our bass player, and his wife were staying in one of those reconverted houses that let out rooms to musicians. In those days there weren't many people outside the entertainment field renting rooms to us. Musicians were considered disreputable, always in transit, in town for a week and out, gigs folding, drinking and gambling their wages away and likely as not to run out on the bill. So when you were on the road and couldn't find a motel that would accept you, you'd seek out a brother—in every sizable town there were always a few cats playing our music and we'd find each other—and the grapevine would alert you to the people who had houses specifically for musicians to stay. Rooms across from each other, toilet down the hall, and a community kitchen where you could cook and save money. It was in one of those kitchens that Frank Clarke came to grief: some funny little argument over running too much hot water with a bitch who phoned her brother across the bay, told him Frank pushed her around. Her brother came into town that afternoon, rang the bell and asked for Frank. When Frank came to the door, her brother pulled out his pistol and blew Frank's brains out right there on the steps. The band served as pallbearers and Jack McVea started drinking and crying—went on for three days so it was that long before we worked again. Three months after the shooting Frank's widow called me in Los Angeles, said she was going to get married again and did I think it too soon, would it look funny Frank not even cold in the grave and all? I told her what I thought Sevener might have told her, that the time element didn't make any difference, he's gone and you got to live your life so if this is what you want, go ahead and do it; makes a lot more sense than sittin' around the house grievin'. They're still together in San Francisco after twenty-three years, but I sometimes think back to that time when I was barely twenty and wonder what business I had giving out advice like that.

Miles Davis had come to town and began playing at the Oasis and other clubs. He was a dentist's son out of East St. Louis and had gone to the Juilliard School in New York. That was some heavy shit; not many cats were going to music schools in those days. But good music doesn't necessarily come out of that kind of knowledge so he went into the streets. Since he couldn't play high like Dizzy he compensated by picking all the pretty notes—got strong out of his weakness— and later blazed his own trail.

In the spring of 1950 I was staying at Rufus Brown's house in San Francisco while working a gig across the Bay. Rufus was a pimp and sold dope, and his old lady was a whore. He gave musicians one flat price that included room, meals, and dope, considerately running the last item on the cuff, marking down the number of fixes (for which we'd line up after meals downstairs in his pad) and settling accounts at the end of each week. One of the older musicians in the house used to cap on me* in a playful way, saying, Your hair sure looks good, how come you look so slick all the time? Though I was getting strung I was always appearance-conscious in those early years, wouldn't consider leaving for work without a trim haircut, clean white shirt and tie. For a month I stayed with Rufus and his woman, eating, working my gig, and shooting dope. There would be lean times ahead when I wasn't working and I was beginning to feel the first cold shadow of the Man who has your destiny in his hands, and the constant need I would have to keep from getting sick. In the years ahead I would hustle and scheme like a motherfucker and sometimes think that if I had directed all that drive and con into legitimate channels, I might be worth a cool million today.

That summer when I came home I knew I was in serious trouble. I said to Sevener, "I got a friend in Mexico I'm going to stay with awhile, I'm sick." He said, "Well, I'll give you some milk of magnesia." *Motherfucker, I'm using heroin, I got a two-year habit, what you talkin' about milk of magnesia?* I tried again, "Daddy, you don't understand, I'm feelin' bad, flashes 'n' things in front of my eyes. I don't know what's happening to me." And he said, "Well, son, you might be goin' crazy."

* Put me down.

8

Meet Me in Albuquerque

It was at Wardell's wife's house that I met Jackie Clag-ett. She worked as a teller in the Security First National Bank, had grown up apart from the community of night people, but had gone through some shit of her own, had a little devilment in her, and I guess that, along with her looks, was what attracted me. She must have felt the kindredness, too, otherwise she probably would have ended up marrying a dentist or the head teller in the bank or some other goody two-shoes.

I didn't see her again for a couple of months after that first meeting, until the night she and Wardell's wife and another girl friend came to hear me play at The Flame. After the gig we stood around outside talking for a while, then as Jackie was driving away her girl friend said, Aren't you going to kiss her good-bye? It didn't seem like too bad an idea, so I did. Two days later I picked her up and took her to a show, along with three friends of mine—that blew her mind a little, she wasn't used to that kind of informality—and that was the start of twenty years of companionship, ups and downs, some sweet times and a lot of turmoil.

We started hanging out; it got serious. I wasn't looking to

get tied down and knew I had to make a move one way or the other. I took her up to my room one night and said, Look, I don't want you hanging around anymore. I'm fucked up, you're taking a big handicap on yourself. She didn't say anything, just looked at me. The piano comes first anyway, I said. I don't even like you, so why don't you just split. She kept on looking at me, hurt and puzzled, so I tied up in front of her. You see this spoon? I said. You know what that stuff is? Heroin. Watch, I said, I'm going to put it in my arm . . . Went through the whole procedure, step by step. It must have been a good performance because after the curtain fell she split and for the next few months didn't phone or try to get in touch with me.

But she kept popping up in different places—somebody's house, an after-hours joint. When summer came she drove to St. Louis on her vacation to visit a girl friend. I got the number, phoned, asked how you doin', what's happenin', trying to keep from telling her how much I missed her. She said she was leaving the next morning, would be in Albuquerque on such and such a day to see her grandmother, why didn't I meet her there as she didn't want to drive home alone over the mountains. I took off a few days from my gig in Palm Springs (could have been Palm Springs, Alabama, for all the use I had of the swimming pool, bar and dining room) and flew to Albuquerque. Arrived in the late afternoon, assuming I would sleep with her that night; it had been a long cold summer. She said, We can't, my grandmother. I said, She's old and half blind, she won't know the difference. She said, It'll look funny. Why funny, I said. We're not married, she said. I slept in her car that night and the next day (dimly aware some kind of intrigue was going down) we drove over the mountains to L.A. Three weeks later we were married by Sevener in the study of his church, attended by my sister Margurite, Wardell and Jackie's father. I couldn't afford a ring so Jackie bought us two gold wedding bands and I contributed my mattress. She had asked her father if it was all right if we lived at his house but if that wasn't cool we'd go someplace else. He said it was okay with him, and when the ceremony was over I drove to my place to pick up my bag and strap my mattress to the roof of the car. He met me at the door, handed me the keys; said, You're home, and an hour later Jackie left with Wardell and me for Oxnard where we were working three nights a week with Scat Man Crothers.

That winter I recorded the first tracks under my own name for Discovery Records—two sides of a 45 single, "Thou Swell" and an original, "Jumping Jacque," dedicated to Jackie—and in the spring Howard McGhee phoned asking me to join his group for a European tour. I said, Groovy, let's go. But then came a counter command from the U.S. government saying I was urgently needed in Korea.

9

The Mariana Islands
Turkey Shoot

Ever since I was a kid reading *Terry and the Pirates* I've always dug uniforms. I dug football uniforms, the clash of team colors against each other, and the heavy German uniforms in World War II movies; I dug braid and insignia, Ike jackets were very cool, and air force suntans. Whenever I drew a picture in school it was of an air force pilot in smart tans with wings and ribbons. My greatest desire was to fly a P-40 over Europe and come back and have my parents say, "You were a bad motherfucker up in that sky." I think deep down I must have been a really patriotic cat. The American flag has always looked groovy to me, though I came to dislike a lot of the people representing it. What screws up the flag too often are the people who try to interpret for everyone else what it stands for. But flags when they're friendly are cool, just like pride is cool, and I believe my fondness for the flag is what put me in the army when I wasn't supposed to go in, when I could have got out easy as running an F7 chord.

I was the only bonafide 4F I knew who got drafted. At Fort

Ord my records somehow got stamped 1A, but when the last doctor saw the scars on my arms he put me on medical hold and sent me to a psychiatrist who asked if I wanted to get out. Now this was 1952 when representing the American flag wasn't that much of a drag. I started thinking about Terry and the Pirates and the flag and said I wasn't all that sure I wanted to get out. He left it up to me, told me if I thought I was going to make it, okay, but if I thought I was going to get fucked up and strung out again, which I eventually did, then I ought to split. When I finally walked out of there, it hit me like the Santa Ana wind. I could have got out. Shit, I didn't want to go anywhere, I just wanted to play music. But for some crazy reason—and as I look back I was completely crazy in 1952 (it was almost *fashionable* to be crazy then, musicians would go around saying "Catch that crazy motherfucker" and it was like a badge of praise)—I kept walking in a daze down that hot dusty road straight into the army.

My first night at Ord a sergeant and a drummer I knew said they were going to San Francisco and did I want to come. I hadn't been assigned or even issued a uniform yet and was supposed to stay on base, but I knew I could cop* up there and I'd heard Bird was in town so there'd be some music too. Fuck it, I said, let's go. A hundred yards out the gate I had a feeling the sergeant was juiced, the impression confirmed a mile further on when the jeep took a funny turn like it was on tracks and the switchman had fucked up, sailed through some trees over a ten-foot incline and began rolling over. On the first turnover my hand went through the windshield, sliced to the bone, and on the second or third the drummer's collarbone

* Buy dope.

gave. Sergeant got up and walked away from it with a scratch on his chin like he was strolling out of the can, nicked himself shaving. It was an early omen of things to come.

After 4 weeks of basic I was assigned to the heavy weapons company—bazookas, mortars and such, all the really heavy shit you bring to bear on the enemy. As a kid I had hunted jackrabbits and quail summers with Sevener at Lake Elsinore, so I knew how to shoot. First week on the range my platoon officer, a skinny old cracker from Texas who didn't take much to niggers but appreciated a good shot said, "Hawes, how come you shoot so straight, you're supposed to play that boogie-woogie. You keep hittin' that bull's-eye like you were one of Nimitz's boys at the Mariana Islands turkey shoot." I wound up with the highest score on the range and won one of those medals with the metal piece dangling from a colored ribbon that means you're a slick motherfucker. I loved to shoot and when I soldiered, I soldiered. I never have dug war, but if I'd made it to the front lines in Korea and those suckers had made one of their banzai charges, I probably would've 'offed* my share before they finally got me.

Whenever I had a pass I'd go to L.A. or San Francisco to cop and jam. Bird was working at Jimbo's, an after-hours club in San Francisco, at the time and if he knew I was looking to score he'd say in his stagey, put-on way, "I haven't messed with anything along those lines in a long while, but what I can do is make a call for you . . ." He'd see me at Jimbo's later— from two in the morning on was the heavy time, when the cats would get off their gigs and come to jam and the chicks would show—and say, "The cat's out in the alley, you can cop for

* Killed.

twenty-five cents." * I'd say I didn't have twenty-five cents, which may not have been true. Usually I'd already copped, could have used more, but I knew there was a good chance Bird might burn me—knew what *I* might have done in similar circumstances. If I said, "I only need a dime's worth," he'd say, "Well, I'm low myself, make it two dimes and we'll cow." ** Of course if I went for that it was unlikely I'd ever see that second dime. It was survival of the fittest in those days and you had to know where people were coming from. Lenny Bruce was working San Francisco at the same time and when we were both low on bread, which was a good part of the time, we'd meet someplace to cow and tie up together.

From heavy weapons I was transferred to band training: marching in a field like at football half time, learning the general protocol, the ruffles and flourishes. The officers in charge didn't know shit about our music, which was a drag, otherwise it might not have been too bad a way to pass the days. It was about this time I started fucking up. Be on a pass in L.A. or San Francisco and lose track of the time; look at my watch and say, Damn, I'm in the army, gotta get back. The third time I showed late they shot me back to the heavy weapons company, and when the 16-week period was up assigned me to the 49th Army Band at Camp Irwin in Barstow. Right, Route 66. Kingman, Barstow, San Bernadino. More parades and marches. Sad-ass tunes like the Colonel Bogey March. Piano players are usually assigned glockenspiels, but after a week marching crooked with that motherfucker in front of my eyes I was issued cymbals, sometimes a bass drum or snare.

* Twenty-five dollars.
** Pool resources to buy dope.

I managed it for another couple of weeks until a new band-leader took over—sad old cracker out of Tennessee—then I went AWOL.

Back in L.A. I began gigging and recording around town like I was a civilian again, using heavily and getting nervous. One day while Jackie was at work a well-known ofay singer—I'll call her Judy Wells—came over to the house to cop. (Judy was so strung at the time, so pressed for bread, she would often hustle drinks between sets in the clubs where she was appearing. You'd walk in and here's this fine bitch with her name on the marquee outside, winning critics' polls every year, carrying a tray and a bar rag, wiping tables. When it came time for her show she'd disappear into the dressing room and come back out in a black taffeta dress, her hair pinned up. Lights would go down and the man would say, "The Blue Eagle Inn takes enormous pride in presenting the fabulous Judy Wells." Jekyll and Hyde had nothing on Judy in those days.) We were in the midst of our transaction when the doorbell rang. I peeked out the curtains and saw two police, one with a black book in his hand. They were nice looking young cops and re-minded me of the pair who had come to the house when I was fifteen because some neighbors had complained I was disturb-ing the peace, practicing the piano late at night. They had stood on the porch for ten minutes listening before ringing the bell, they said, and I must have some pretty funny neighbors complaining about music like that; but better use the soft pedal. (I remember thinking, If I can charm a pair of ofay cops for ten minutes on a front porch I might really have some-thing.) I looked at that black book now and figured it couldn't be anything more serious than a traffic warrant—I'd been picking up tickets easy as gum wrappers lately—but I was in no mood to deal with that shit and shot out the back. Judy, who is known in the business for her cool head under fire, told me the following exchange went down:

"Is Mr. Hawes in?"

"No."

"Do you know when he'll be back?"

"He's on tour in the Midwest."

"Who are you?"

"The maid."

I waited twenty minutes before I came back in. Twenty—not fifteen. With enough experience you get so you can *deduce* the set of logical deductions which cops make: *Something fishy here. Let's give this spade fifteen minutes.* And they sit in their car at the corner for a quarter hour watching the house. What you have to do is break their pattern and then you can usually manage to stay a step ahead.

Jackie and my sisters tried to get me to go back to camp. Took me to the terminal and put me on the bus three times, but when they got home I was already there: beat them back in a cab. My sister Margurite said, Next time you get off that bus I'm gonna turn you into the MP's. And the following day when an officer came from camp, a cat I knew and liked, and assessed the situation for me—*If you're still here tomorrow when I return, I'm going to have to bust you and I don't want to*—I knew it was time I was getting back.

I had been gone over a month. Went straight to the base hospital and told the doctor, I'm fucked up. He took one look and agreed. Put me to bed under guard and fed me demerol for two weeks. The CID* dropped by to ask where I was getting it. I said, Just stand on any corner in L.A. and look

* Civilian Investigation Department.

funny. When the hospital commander, who was a lieutenant colonel, found out I was a musician, he began dropping by afternoons with his trumpet. I had to play with him though he was the sorriest hornman I think I ever heard.

I was court-martialed and given ninety days. The first week on detail I was painting a fence with some other prisoners when a cracker guard from Mississippi in a Frank Buck helmet got on my case.* It must have been 100 degrees in the barracks' shade that day and I guess all the shit I'd been through suddenly weighed down and I snapped: grabbed the guard's rifle and busted him in the side of the head with the butt; might have killed the motherfucker if the other prisoners hadn't grabbed me. From that point my troubles started in earnest.

There's an open-air solitary confinement facility in the Mojave Desert that as you approach from a distance looks like a corral for horses in an old Tex Ritter movie. Only as you get closer do you see the four small guard towers. After three days laying on a board under the July sun my face was covered with blisters and my lips looked like a tribal priest's in a grass hut village. The chaplain came by, took one look and said, Cut this man loose. Forthwith. Back at Irwin I lay around the base hospital for ten days with vaseline on my face. I wrote Jackie, told her what had gone down, and she phoned the commanding general. Must have really shook him up, because when the scabs dropped off and I started looking human again they put me on a bus to Fort Ord so fast they forgot to send my records. (Not long afterward I heard that the CO who had court-martialed me had dropped dead of a heart attack. I felt kind of sorry for the dude, but at the same time it did seem like a natural pattern of justice was at work.)

* Harassed me.

I served the rest of my sentence in the Fort Ord stockade. After two weeks I was made trustee; phoned Jackie and told her she could come up and visit me, which she'd been doing pretty regularly the times I wasn't in a stockade. The next morning I received orders to report to Camp Stoneham, the port of embarkation. When Jackie arrived she told me her allotment checks weren't coming through. I told her everything's fucked up, the motherfuckers are sending me to Korea. She was sorry to hear that, she said, but you're so damn crazy you'll probably capture the whole Chinese army by mistake looking for dope.

10

Ambassador

My records kept on getting messed up. By the time I boarded ship for Korea I'd been AWOL so many times and served time in so many different stockades there was bound to be a lag in the paper work. Forty of us were marched to the boat under shotgun guard. When the boarding officer came to me he looked at his list and said, "Who the hell are you?" I said, "Shit, man, you ought to know, you put me on the boat." He said, "You can't go to Korea, I don't have your records." I said, "Well I'm here, what do you want me to do?" and he said, "Don't worry about it."

They put us, the forty under guard, down in the hold, and about the time the boat was passing under the Golden Gate Bridge a navy officer came down and said, "Gentlemen, welcome back to the United States Army." All I could think of was if only I'd been in the air force with my wings I'd probably end up a colonel and groove right through to the end of the war. After a while they let us up on deck and when we looked back, there was San Francisco no bigger than a thimble. What they were telling us in effect was, okay, you free, go jump off the deck if you think you can swim. One day out of

San Francisco the truce was signed and our destination was changed to Japan.

Yokohama Bay was so filled with ships it was like a toy armada floating in a bathtub. There was no parking space at the piers so we had to stay anchored overnight. They showed a movie, but most everyone stayed on deck staring at the shore lights and talking about one thing: *Think of all those Japanese broads waiting for us, we could be screwing like mad.* I went along with them, agreeing, Right, you right, Jim, crazy bitches, never had no Japanese ass, but what I was thinking was, *This is the Orient, man, there has got to be a lot of groovy dope in that town.*

Most of the soldiers I'd been in the stateside stockades with were shipped to Pusan, but as they didn't have any records or orders on me, no indication of what my training was, I was sent to Camp Drake, a replacement center in the town of Asaka, which was cool; they had Japanese cats doing KP and chicks on the gate as interpreters. As I was getting only partial pay because of the records mix-up, bread became an immediate problem. The first night at Drake I decided with three other cats to check how cool the security was and see if we could get into town to score. We threw some dufflebags filled with army blankets and other contraband over a dark part of the fence, followed the bags over and right away saw security wasn't all that bad. Ali of a sudden it's Central Avenue on Saturday night. Flashlights poking our faces, lot of little cats in blue uniforms and blue helmets milling around, jabbing shotguns at us, talkin' about HALT. Now at the time we were occupying Japan, their soldiers weren't supposed to shoot ours, so it was likely their guns weren't loaded; but in the heat of the moment it didn't occur to any of us to test that theory out.

They herded us through the gate and delivered us to the MP's who kept us overnight. The next morning a captain just back from Korea with a chestful of medals told us we must be either crazy or stupid to do such a dumb thing—the stupidness seemed to bother him more than anything else—why didn't we run? We said we thought the guns might be loaded. He said, See that building over there? You want to mop it from top to bottom or you want a court-martial? We said, You're gonna see the cleanest motherfucking building in the whole goddamn Orient. He was an ofay, but a nice cat, had faced death for over a year and couldn't be bothered too much with petty infractions. It was late summer, bone dry and hot as a bitch, and I heard he made himself a small bundle selling black market Coca-Cola before returning to the States.

On my first legal pass, shoes shined and pants creased like any sharp potato-fed U.S. soldier, I split from the group heading for the town bars (have a beer and ball a Japanese broad was the plan for the day) wondering how I was going to score. All my life I'd heard from junkies that dope in Japan and China was it. (Which shows you how stupid the army is. They knew I'd been strung so why send me to the place where all the best shit is?) Now at the time I wasn't strung. I had a habit when I entered the army, kicked, but every time I was AWOL or home on a pass I'd use. But with the time in the stockades and the boat trip it had been some three months since I'd used.

I started walking into town along some rice paddies trying to figure out a course of action. I knew I couldn't stop some strange cat on the street and ask because—number one, there was the language barrier, and two, I was smart enough to know there were probably some undercover CID people around. My mind was just focusing on the idea of *sin*—where there's one kind of sin there's usually another, *i.e.,* a whorehouse was the thing—when like a genie out of a bottle a little old cat popped out in the road in front of me. Strange genie wearing a kind of hip hat, funny raincoat and tennis shoes. He said in broken English, "Hey, where you goin' to?" Just goin', I said. "You want nice girl?" Okay.

He trotted down the road ahead of me and the next thing I knew I was sitting in a house on a bamboo bench and Mama-san is parading some sharp groovy chicks in kimonos before me, bowing and smiling, doing their part to get me excited. I turned down the first chick and Mama-san brought on two others, equally fine, opening their kimonos and flipping their breasts around so I could appreciate their youthfulness and spring. I said I didn't want them either. By this time everyone's looking at me funny, thinking this dude's got to be in the wrong pad, must be looking for a nice, fat Japanese boy, and I'm losing heart too. But when the sliding door opened to admit the fourth chick I happened to glance down the hall and saw a skinny bitch pushing a broom. I almost fell out. Felt my face break into a big happy grin because even at a distance I could see that this chick's arms look like the Penn Central switching yards. I'd never seen arms with that many scars, could hardly conceive of anyone pumping up their veins so bad. She was emaciated, couldn't have weighed more than eighty pounds; her jaw was sunken, there were dark circles around her eyes and it was understandable why they had her pushing a broom. No soldiers were going to pay any kind of bread for her, so if you can't fuck at least keep the place clean. When I saw that mess of tracks I said to Mama-san, That's it, that's who I want. She looked back at the broompusher, then at me, puzzled because I'm the most unlikely-looking junkie she ever saw; I've been eating three squares a day, plenty of army potatoes, and am coming on fat and sassy. Suddenly she's all in a sweat, batting her eyes and fluttering her fat hands, Oh no, bad girl, not good girl for you—so I figured the ultimate thing to do to close the deal is to bring out my wallet. Mama-san glanced at my bread and I knew if I'd said right there I wanted to screw the bamboo bench I was sitting on she would have given me the bench to screw. Ah-so. She went down the hall to tell the broompusher she's it, and that bitch's eyes lit up; she must have thought Buddha's elevated her back to the good graces and done sent her somebody to love. Dropped the broom, happy as a kid, and went running into a nearby room. You wait, Mama-san said, she'll prepare for you. I didn't need anyone preparing for me, but I didn't want to give my game away. Let her put on the powder and lipstick and whatever else, do the whole thing. I'd waited this long anyway. When she was ready I went down the hall into the room, and even as I pulled her into a corner and whispered in her ear, "Ahen (heroin), she kept smiling and bowing, thanking Buddha for relieving her of the broom, putting her back in harness. I had to say again, "Ahen," and it must be very hard for an Oriental chick's eyes to get round but suddenly this eighty-pound Japanese bitch is Orphan Annie backing away from me frightened and cowering against the wall, those moon eyes taking in a healthy potato-fed American soldier, wondering since when's the CIA hire nigger undercover agents. I rolled up my left sleeve to show her and now there were moons within moons. Ah-so. Soldier shoot up? You dumb bitch, what do you think I been trying to tell you for the past minute? She took me to the window which looked out on a kind of courtyard and signaled to the little genie in the hip hat and tennis shoes who was squatting down in the dirt doing something to a bicycle. He came over, she jabbered a few sentences at him, slipped him some of my loot and in no time the little guy had cycled off, copped and was back with the shit.

Now this chick who's been on a broom for months, wasted, probably having to steal what little dope she got, is so goddamned happy to have found a friend she's laughing and kidding around, hitting me on the arm, and I'm as happy as her, I've got it, found my source, we're like two kids racing across a meadow with bright balloons and she's getting the accessories out of a bureau drawer, being very careful with the amount of shit she's allotting me, doling the stuff onto a crushed cigarette package shaped to a tiny basin and adding water, she doesn't want to lose me, knows I'll be back, scared I might die in this goddamn place six thousand miles from Central Avenue. "Aren't you going to cook it?" I ask. She doesn't know what I'm talking about. I'm thinking, How can this bitch have all those tracks and not even know how to cook it? No cookie in Japan, she finally gets across to me, just draw it up straight ahead and shoot. *Use more.* No-no-no, too strong. *Listen, do you think this is the first time I shot shit? I've been shooting shit from Watts to 130th Street* (letting her know what a bad cat I am), *come on, shake it out.* No-no, too much. *Will you listen to me, I'll shoot Unguentine, battery water, don't make no difference—it's my money, if I die, I die, fuck it, Fats Navarro went down, we ain't no super race* . . . Please-no, I like you. *I like you too, baby, but I want to get tore up!* . . . We compromised, she shook out a little more then squatted down in front of me, her kimono parting—not all that bad, I thought and made a mental note, One of these days I'm going to ball this bitch but for right now let's get high. She tied the tourniquet, looking at me, still fearful and I'm saying, *Bitch, will you please shoot this shit in my arm and stop bullshitting.* She stuck the needle in, jacked it off so the blood came in, shot it, and I'm about to say, "This shit ain't nothin'." I looked in those dark-ring almond eyes and said, "This shit ain't . . ." And it was all over. Over and out. After all that conniving and pleading, going through all those changes to get a fix. When I woke up, the whole family, Mama-san, Poppa-san who had come in, couple little kids, all the young fine chicks and my bitch were sitting around in a circle fanning me, saying, "Yes . . . ah-so . . ." Groovy.

Then and there I became the best damn ambassador for the United States. The American image over there at the time was soldiers balling Japanese daughters, buying beer, drop a kid a quarter for a shoeshine, four-star suckers walking around showing off the stars and stripes and generally trying to lead these Orientals into more affluent ways, right? But I came over with my black ass messed up—just off the boat, my first pass, I go out and make contact—and right away they understood me. Took me into the bosom of their family. See, American soldier fucked up too. That's what gets you across, opens the lines of communication.

The next day when I got my pass and started down the little road past the rice paddies with some pears and candy bars I'd bought, the word had already got around: "Uma-san's coming." (They didn't know how to say "Hawes," it kept coming out "Horse," so rather than offend me they hit on "Uma-san," as "uma" is Japanese for horse.) "Uma-san's coming." Little kids on bicycles met me halfway. Mama-san

greeted me at the door saying, "Ah, ah-so, Uma-san." I hugged
her and said, "Where's my woman?" She was in back getting
prettied up, happily putting on her powder and lipstick. So
I lay around the parlor sharing my pears and candy while
Mama-san and Poppa-san brought in grapes and other goodies.
Here was a house of prostitution and they were treating me
like a son, like King Farouk. But you know when the sliding
door opened and my queen came in, skinny as a stalk, her
little sunken face snow white against ruby lips and dark eyes,
I glanced past her down the hall and saw one of those fine
sharp bitches I'd turned down yesterday. Damn if they didn't
have her on the broom.

A junkie from Harlem I'll call Cornelius was part of
the permanent staff at Drake. Had a big 2 on him, Second
Army. He was a cadre and his job was to greet the cats coming
from the States: *"Leave your shit over there, chow's at five
o'clock, you'll report over here for barracks and duty assign-
ments . . ."* We started hanging out together and after a while
he made me his assistant; that way I could go out on pass every
day to cop. Cornelius would line up 800 cats and say, "CO be
out here in a minute to talk to you, stand at ease, the smoking
lamp is lit." Then he'd give me a look and I'd wander over to
the barracks and fill a dufflebag with cameras. We'd meet a
little later and he'd say, How'd we do? I'd say, We're cool. Our
Japanese source would be outside the fence and in a minute
we'd have $200–$300 in our pockets and be on our way into
town to get high.
After two months at Drake I was finally given my first duty
assignment: fire guard. That involved walking around the inside of the fence with a flashlight, walking stick, and a helmet

with a white stripe around it. Spot a fire or smell smoke, you pull the alarm. Some of my family from the whorehouse, the little kids and those chicks who weren't working at the time, would walk along outside the fence to keep me company, and whenever I needed some dope and couldn't get away, they'd throw the shit over the fence. One day I walked three shifts, took everybody's duty 'cause I was happy and feeling good and didn't want to go to sleep. Every so often I'd ask for five minutes' release, go in the toilet and fix, come back, put my funny helmet on and start around the fence again, tapping my stick, saluting everybody, Hi, how you doin' . . . Hamp's sure a good soldier, they said, takes care of business; easygoing cat, nothing ruffles him. CO was impressed, wanted to give me a three-day pass. I said, No, it's cool, I'm fine, man.

It was a groovy time of my service career. I was hustling, had my shit together, dough in my pockets. Like I said, when you're strung you can connive like a motherfucker, find yourself tapping unsuspected creative reserves.

One night I played at a Red Cross club and some people said, "Oh, shit, there's a soldier plays good." Somehow word filtered down to Yokohama, where the 289th Army Band was stationed, that there's a jazz musician at Drake who's cut some records and he's not even assigned. So the lines of communication were opened and I was pulled into the army band. It was a sad leavetaking after three months with my adopted family. I thought of all the good days at the pad, the warmth and affection, gettin' high, eatin' grapes, the nights on fire guard, some of my family always on the other side of the fence, walking along with me so I wouldn't get lonely.

The day I left for Yokohama they were all there to see me

off, the chicks and the little kids, Mama-san and Poppa-san, crying and carrying on as if I were being taken away to train as a kamikaze pilot, knowing they weren't ever going to see me again. It got to me so, I started crying too, I'd never known that kind of affection outside of home. Cornelius came down too, shook my hand, said, See you, man, stay cool. (I never did see that dude again, but when I got back to California three years later to serve out a sentence in prison at Lompoc, I found he'd already preceded me there, had been released just a week earlier.) Then the train was ready to leave, I was hugging everyone, my woman was laying a traveling supply on me and I thought, Well, here I go, big city, ready for all that shit again. Because during those three months I had got strung bad and I knew it was serious.

11

Doko-e-ikima-su-ka?

Day after I arrived at Camp Zama the *Stars and Stripes* came out with my picture on the front: *Famous Jazz Pianist From Los Angeles Joins 289th Army Band.* CO went around grinning all day, "See the paper yet? . . . How about that?" like I was Sousa come back from the grave. There were two main bands in Japan: the headquarters band in Tokyo that played all the heavy events—top brass arriving from the States and Europe, receptions for heads of state, ambassadors, congressmen—and our group in Yokohama. Actually we had the better musicians but they had the sparkle and prestige, so we were considered the peasant outfit. The Yokohama CO wanted to make his band as heavy as Tokyo's so my arrival put a little feather in his cap, though he didn't realize at the time that feather was so small it would hardly tickle a fly.

My third night in Yokohama I saw two soldiers nodding in a service club and said to myself, Something's happening here.

With my first pass I wandered into town along one of the main streets, down a line of bright neon bars, the lights wavering through the fog like streaks of lime and lemon paint in a greasy river. Picked up on some high-pitched female cussing

60

through a doorway and out of one of those bars came a chick looking like Suzie Wong, the hippest, baddest whore on the block, fine, tall and strutting proud.

She called to me from across the street, "Hey, soldier, doko-e-ikima-su-ka?"

I knew what that sounded like and just kept on walking.

"Doko-e-ikima-su-ka?"

Kept walking.

"Hey, motherfucker, where you goin'?"

Now I stopped. Faced this bitch across the street in her tight shiny skirt, hands on hips, feisty-looking like she owned the whole block, and said, "Goin' to get high."

She smiled and said, "You don't know, do you?"

I said, "Do you?"

She said, "You bet your ass. C'mon."

"I'm comin'."

So I'd found me another friend. How was I to know "doko-e-ikima-su-ka" meant "where you goin'?"

I said, "What's your name?"

"Be-bop."

"What're you talkin' about, you don't know nothin' about any be-bop."

"I know who Bird and Dizzy are."

"Now how could you know them, sittin' way over here all your life eatin' rice 'n shit?" Excited and nervous, I said, "You've never had any black-eyed peas, you don't know anything about any goddamn blues," totally naive, you dig, about across-the-sea lines of communication in this field.

"Why should you know about them and not me?" she said.

" 'Cause I'm a damn musician, that's why."

This blew her mind. She said, "I'll take you to the Harlem

Club where there's a girl Toshiko plays like Bud Powell."

Harlem Club? Bud Powell? She had to be coming out of some funny bag or I was dreaming. "Carry on, Suzie," I said, "take me to your Harlem Club, then we'll cop."

I sat in the back of the club with her watching Knobby Totah, an Arabian bass player I'd just met in the Zama band, warm up. The drummer joined him and then this little chick in a kimono sat down at the piano and started to rip off things I didn't believe, swinging like she'd grown up in Kansas City.

"See what I mean?" Be-bop said.

I'm thinking, What's this bitch doing over here playing so natural and authentic so far away.

After the set she came over with Knobby and said, "You're Hampton Hawes, I was hoping you'd come by." And the next thing she said as we shook hands was, "Have you ever met Bud Powell?" I said, "No, but I know what you mean, I can tell by the way you play."

It shook me up, the sounds were filtering out from the States over oceans, across rice paddies. These Asians knew about Bird and Dizzy and Bud and all the time I'd thought nobody past 52nd Street or Central Avenue could possibly be hip to them.

The next night to celebrate our meeting she arranged a big dinner for me and Knobby and her trio. Seemed like a banquet, ten courses, different bottles of wine and about five waiters hovering around us. When it was over I took out my wallet and said, "We better go Dutch," but she just smiled across the table at me and said, "Everything's cool. Welcome to Japan."

At Zama I set myself up pretty good from the start. Had a permanent pass which meant that as long as I made roll call (although $5 could usually buy you a stand-in and some mornings there'd be as few as thirty-five cats standing in that gray light answering for 175 names) and showed up on time for work—receptions at the service clubs and playing ships in at the port—I was free. I kept a uniform in one of those ten-cent lockers at the port and when it came time to play in the USS So-and-So I'd go down there, change, play the gig, then change back into my civvies and be set for the night in Yokohama.

I started hanging out at the Harlem Club which was run by Ray Bass, an American brother, and Toshiko and I became tight, grooving and playing for each other. She was a big star in Japan at the time; if gospel had been as big as jazz, she would have been Sister Rosetta Tharpe or Aretha Franklin. At first I thought she was only hanging out with me to talk about Bud, to be close to the source. I had recorded, was getting known in the States, and if I wasn't Bud Powell I was maybe two or three grooves removed from him which was the closest she was going to get. What she probably didn't realize was how good she played, so she didn't really need me in that respect. Later on she made it on her own in the States. Anyway I soon discovered she dug me for myself and we developed a lasting friendship. The American consulate arranged for us to play a concert together and the response was so good they contacted the army to see about sending us on tour—Toshiko in her kimono, me in my slick American uniform—figuring it might help improve relations between the two countries which were touchy at the time with the occupation still on. But somebody squashed the idea, probably one of those cracker Texas colonels; which shows you how thin the knife edges are in life. If the scales had tipped a little bit to the left I might have got myself cleaned up and come back a hero, picture on the cover of *Jet* and *Newsweek* (*Soldier singlehandedly cements Orient ties*), instead of as a miserable strung-out prisoner. Might still be in the service today, two stars on my shoulder and going for more, standing on some air base tarmac, tall and proud, razor creases on my pants, raft of ribbons gleaming on my chest, welcoming the POW's back.

Word was filtering in about the 25th Infantry Division. This was a mixed black-and-white outfit headed by a Kentucky colonel and the word was there was so much dope going around that the medics had to shoot salt in the veins of practically the whole division to get them up for reveille; that during the Korean action the colonel often had to slow them down (*As of 1300 hours you crazy bastards are five miles ahead of the whole Eighth Army, but you'll never read about it back home!*); and that one night when the Chinese made a banzai charge on them the motherfuckers came out of their foxholes and banzaied back so fierce the Chinese dropped their guns and ran like wild turkeys being shot at in Tennessee. Now some people thought the stories were mostly jive, but knowing what good Oriental junk can do for you I tended to accept them as gospel.

When it really hit me that the amount of shit in circulation was much greater than I'd expected was the afternoon we were getting ready to play a parade and I noticed the platoon sergeant sitting on a bunk looking funny. Nice ofay cat, a career soldier and drummer in the band; had his wife and kids living just outside the base. I said, Man, what's wrong with you, you got a cold? He said, I wish it was a cold. I looked at him close and said, Man, are you fucked up? He looked up and said, Yeah, and I said, Well follow me down the road to the bathroom and I will help you out.

It was a big parade that day. A week earlier the Communists had had their May Day parade during which Yokohama had been off-limits to all American personnel, and now the Nationalists were doing their stuff and we were helping them celebrate, moving down the main drag of Yokohama under a bright, hot sky in our slick scarves and silver helmets. I'm clashing my cymbals, watching the sergeant a row ahead rattling his sticks, funny little smile on his face, and thinking, That dude sure had me fooled, if all these Joe Palooka and Clark Kent type cats are fucked up maybe there's some hope for the world, There are so many units ahead of us—it's like Rose Bowl day in Pasadena—we're hardly moving, and that sun's blazing brighter every minute. A block farther on my uniform is soaked with sweat and I know I'm going to be sick before this motherfucker is over—realizing at the same time that I'd given all my shit to the sergeant. Ten minutes go by, we've moved maybe another block. Sweat's pouring out of the helmet down my face like someone had filled a derby with water in a Three Stooges movie, the cymbals are feeling like fifty-pound barbells and I'm telling myself, I'll never make it, when I spot a familiar-looking house on the right, Mama-san in the doorway. Said to the bass drummer, I'll be right back, and moved sideways out of ranks, still banging my cymbals, through the curb spectators parting like I'm Moses and they're the Red Sea, past Mama-san and on into the house. Her eyes are big with fright, she's staring at the cymbals and silver helmet probably thinking, Must be some kind of weird MP; then she looks closer and says, Oh, it's you, what's goin' on? I say, If you don't give me some shit inside of five seconds you're gonna have a dead soldier layin' across your feet. I fixed in a back room, put the extra shit in my pocket, came back out and saw my row was less than a half block away. Recrossed the Red Sea and eased back into line crashing the cymbals. The bass drummer said, You must be crazy, I never seen anyone do that before in my life. I said, Neither have I, everything's cool. On to Pasadena. Who'd you say UCLA was playing?

The Mama-sans and whores all seemed to like me and would go out of their way to help me. I don't know why except they knew I was crazy and messed up and maybe they had a sentimental feeling for me. They were really the only close friends I had. Be-bop was my main savior those months in Yoke.* She turned out to be just what I thought she was when I saw her that first night through the fog in her shiny silk skirt: the baddest strung-out whore on the block, the proudest one and the feistiest. I'd get tricks for her and she'd use part of the bread to cop for us both. When the cats came from Korea on R & R, I'd say, You want to meet the finest broad in Yokohama? Then I'd just walk them into the club and they'd pull out their wallets so fast the bills and cards would spill to the floor. I suppose you could say I was her pimp, but we were strung bad and she didn't want either of us to get sick. It was a convenient working arrangement. After we'd been together for almost two months she said, You know, Hampton, you've been awful nice to me and never tried to touch me. But I sometimes forget I'm a woman with you so if you ever want to fuck me you can.

I did, a week or two later. It was cool.

I was using so much I knew it was just a matter of time before I started messing up. I had been put in charge of the jazz

* Yokohama.

band. No stripes, everyone else in the group outranked me, but for two hours a day they were on call for rehearsal and took their orders from me. It wasn't a bad little band. We had stock arrangements with grade school chords and voicings and I showed them how to play better harmonies so we would sound hipper. Even the old fatback career sergeants started to dig it. When we played for a dance or show it got off the ground and the reception was generally good. But little things started cropping up. Playing a parade with the marching band I'd find I had on argyle socks with a brown uniform. Leading the jazz band at a concert attended by two- and three-star generals, I saw the CO staring at me from the wings, his face green, and discovered I'd left my insignia and brass, all polished, back on the dresser; I was working that top priority gig in a blank uniform. Little things that I seemed to have no control over. Promoted to PFC (blowing the minds of 99 percent of the band) I sewed on my stripes pointing up like air force V's instead of down; captain took one look at my sleeve and said, Bye. Word started spreading around official quarters to be careful of Hawes, cat might do anything, put him to your pay-him-no-mind list. (Looking back on that time I think their attitude probably was, We can't be too rough on him because he might not know what he's doing.) I wasn't messing up in any obvious standout way, you understand, but neither was I taking care of business, because most every night after work I'd pick up Be-bop and we'd go over to her house and get tore up.

A letter came from Jackie saying the FBI had paid a couple of visits to the house. Seems the paper work had got so far out of hand because of all those AWOL's that I was still listed as a deserter in L.A., which explained a lot of things: Jackie's missing allotment checks and my fucked-up pay and other records. She told them, if he's a deserter then you better check out the imposter playing cymbals with the 289th marching band in Yokohama. A couple of weeks later my records finally arrived along with accumulated back pay of $600. In one lump sum. Well, you *know* I got high that night.

For some time I had known the CID was growing suspicious, but I couldn't help myself. The guys in my outfit dug what was coming down and tried to protect me. Whenever an obvious undercover CID was assigned to the barracks or an investigator called to check on me, the cats in the band, even my sergeant and commanding officer, would clam up, then shoot it back to me: the CID is hip to you, Hampton, be cool. Everyone was nice, wanting to help. But I was too far gone, there was really nothing I could do.

One night after playing at Ray Bass' Harlem Club I was up in Be-bop's second-story pad with a soldier on R & R. As usual wearing my low quarters instead of boots, because you have to take your shoes off to enter a Japanese house and if I wanted to beat a quick retreat I wouldn't have time to be tying no boots. And this particular house had been staked out before. We were getting into things pretty good when a little kid came tearing by on his bicycle shouting up, "MP comin', MP comin'!" I think I know why our army had so much trouble with secrecy leaks in Vietnam: those Asian kids on their cycles are bitches as watchouts. Many's the time I've known about the approach of the MP's or CID minutes before they arrived. But this kid tonight was a shade slow. He jumped off his cycle, ran into the house yelling, "MP comin'!" and no more than ten seconds behind him the door came crashing down. I got into my low quarters and jumped out the window, landing on the roof of the one-story house next door. Went through the roof thinking, Everybody got to die, all kinds of casualties on the road to truth, and came down in the kitchen with a lot of splintered wood and sawdust. Woman at the stove standing there staring at me like she's thinking, What's it doing raining niggers? I got up, brushed myself off, said "Go mena si" (sorry) and split.

Now to show how insane I was, I ran down the alley and out into the street feeling peaceful and cool because I still had my pass. Watched from a distance the jeeps and flashlights slashing at crazy angles and said to myself, I'll just go back down there and check things out. Strolled back to where I'd just run from, casual, like a spectator, ready to say, What's goin' on? What you do, find some GI's or somethin'? A lot of time seemed to have elapsed. When I reached the house everyone had gone—jeeps, flashlights, everything human and mechanical had split. Wandered through the empty ground-floor rooms, saw a couple of ounces of shit by a hibachi someone had missed, pocketed it and calm as a deacon during vespers wandered back out.

Maybe a week or two later as I was coming back from chow the sergeant said, "CO wants to see you, Hampton." "Okay." When I walked in the barracks the CO was standing by my foot locker with two cats, one of them in civvies. They wanted to take me in for a urinalysis. The CO, still protecting me, said, "Are you following procedure? This man has his rights." "Let's go," the CID said. "Go along with them, Hampton, they'll bring you back," the good CO said.

Even before the results of the urinalysis were in I gave myself away, got sick in the lockup overnight and they had to take me to the hospital in Yokohama. Wasn't any use; no way in the world now I could say, What's all this shit about, nothing's wrong with me, man. When I woke the next morning they gave me morphine and put me in the nut ward. Somehow whenever I'm in that ward I always get put in with an alcoholic. True to form, that afternoon they brought in a nice-looking white kid, blue eyes and blond hair, maybe just married, baby on the way, home every weekend on pass to have Sunday dinner with the folks and in-laws—looking so blond and all-American, like Terry and the Pirates except his eyes were fucked up. When we were alone he looked at me with his fucked-up blue eyes and begged me to help him because there was a damn rooster in bed with him wearing tennis shoes.

12

New Faces of 1952

After two weeks on demerol I came back to Zama to wait until the papers were drawn up for my general court martial. Then I was taken to 8th Army Headquarters in Tokyo in a little car driven by a Japanese. The sergeant assigned to guard me—the baton man in the band—was embarrassed at having to wear his side arm with just the two of us in the back seat. When we got under way he slid it under the driver's seat and all the way in talked about Bird, how he'd tried playing alto himself but couldn't quite get the hang of it. In front of Headquarters he strapped the gun back on, straightened his shoulders and took me in.

The lawyer they assigned me—little gray-haired dude with a strange smile, looked like a 1936 editor of *Batman* magazine —talked to the colonels and reported back, It's all straight, you plead guilty and try to stay clean. You'll do a year and get out of the army. I said, It's no use? He said, It's all arranged. He called in as a character witness an air force lieutenant who used to come to the Harlem Club to hear me and Toshiko play, testifying to my importance as a musician in the States. It was a nice speech, they read it into the records—along with testi-

mony from a first sergeant that I was needed in the Zama band
—then the colonels went backstage and talked to themselves
for a minute. Came back—I'm thinking, Damn, all this ceremony when they know what they're going to do—and said,
One year.

Instead of taking me straight to prison, which was the best
and most humane thing they could have done, I was brought
back to Zama while the shit was processed. All the numbers
they were doing on me you'd think it was Captain Queeg's ass
getting canceled instead of Private Hawes'. I waited around
camp for two weeks, growing nervous, trying to figure out
what was happening. Rumor was the CO was maneuvering to
have me stay in the band and do my time at the camp (still
wanting to outshine the Tokyo outfit) and as his wife was the
daughter of the number two man in the Far East Command—
the same 3-star sucker I'd once played a concert for—he
pulled considerable weight. My nerves were fraying bad and
ready to give when somebody slipped up and issued me a three-
day pass. I thought, Ain't this a bitch, must be some weird
patron saint of strung-out musicians watching after me. But
my pay had been suspended, I had no bread. Didn't have to
think twice: smashed the lock on my footlocker so it would
look like it had been broken into, took anything I could carry
in a parcel and headed straight into Yoke and copped.

The day I got back and reported the theft of gear from my
footlocker (even at that late date still hustling, conniving) I
learned that the CO's efforts had failed and I had to go to the
stockade. I knew I couldn't face it. If they'd taken me when
they were supposed to it would have been cool, but now it
meant I'd get sick and have to kick again. I must have looked
pretty sad-ass and bedraggled because the first sergeant said

to go eat some chow and report back. I went in the front of the chow hall, out the back, saw somebody taking off on a motorcycle, jumped on and split back down the road to Yoke.

I thought I'd been gone but a few days this time but they told me later it was more like a month. I remember sleeping in a lot of strange rooms in different houses—the days and nights ran together in a soft blue shadow, but a corner of my mind must have been still alert, steering me away from Be-bop's pad and other places they might think to look for me—walking around garbage cans through alleys and back lanes (noticing my gold wedding band missing, must have sold it for dope), and one day a little kid yelling "MP's!" and Mama-san taking me down to the river where I spent an hour or maybe a day or a week on a sampan under a big hat, tore up. Little brown kid with broken teeth laughing at me while I tried to get across to him that, It's cool, in my country niggers ain't much different than coolies in yours.

The day of apprehension I was in the Harlem Club, one of those places I shouldn't have been, and it's the only day I remember clearly. When I walked in, Ray Bass looked shook. He said, Hampton, you look terrible. Go upstairs and stay away from the window, I'll call your CO. I said, Why do you want to do that? He said, The CO said if you ever show here to tell you the MP's have orders to shoot you on sight. I said, Then I guess I better split. He said, Man, you're a fugitive, they'll shoot you down like a dog, the CO will send somebody to pick you up in an unmarked car and you can surrender voluntarily—Just go upstairs and wait in my office and I'll phone. I went upstairs, saw a camera on a chair, looped it around my neck, jumped out the window onto a tar roof, came down on it on all fours, easy, like a cat, lowered myself down a drain pipe, and calm as any camera-carrying American tourist strolled into the red-light district.

A day or two later I was nodding at a pinball machine in the center of town, minus the camera and $75 out of the $300 still left in my pocket, when a Japanese cat about four feet tall in short pants and combat boots popped up under me and showed me my picture. Soldier come along, please. I thought, I'm Jack Johnson compared to this dude but I don't know any jujitsu and he might be a bad motherfucker. Okay, you got me. He took me to the Japanese police box, the army came in a minute, and this time, my nine lives spent, they took me straight into Tokyo.

The Japanese-built prison run by the 8th Army is known as the Big 8. Cement dungeon, big wall around it. Clanking doors. The cells like old steel ovens with slots; guard comes by four times a day, you hold your hand out the slot and he gives it a tap so he'll know you haven't offed yourself. I was the Man in the Iron Mask. My gig was pulling a big broom in harness around the yard to settle the dirt; tie a bag of oats around my mouth I'd be a donkey.

After five months the Big 8 got so crowded they shipped me back to Lompoc in California to finish my sentence. The cat who issued me my stuff the first day looked at my name and said, You remember Cornelius? I remember, I said. *Stand at ease, the smoking lamp is lit.* He was through here, talked about you all the time, said you were the craziest motherfucker he ever met. You know, he might be right, I said.

In mid-February, 1955, Jackie came in her new Chevy and we drove back to L.A. Car radio was on, chick with a strange vibrato singing something about life is monotonous, life is a drag. Who's that? I said. "Eartha Kitt." Never heard of her,

I said. "She's the big star from *New Faces of 1952*." I watched the trees go by, sun sparkling off California power lines. Glimpse of ocean out past Goleta Point. Go ahead, Eartha, I said. Go on and sing, whoever you are. Sing like a bird. I'm free.

13

Black Wreath

I called up Wardell and said, I'm back.

He said to come on down to the California Club on Santa Barbara Avenue where he was working with his own group. Soon as I saw him I knew he was strung. It shook me up. I said, What happened, man? All those years you were telling me like a big brother to straighten out and I come back and find *you* messed up. In his careful soft-voiced way he was trying to explain when the waitress came and told him he had a long-distance call. He came back after five minutes blinking and fussing with the buttons on his coat. Bird had died in Nica Rothschild's apartment in New York. Went too far out on the limb and it broke. Well, shit, we ain't no super race, none of us going to be here more than twenty minutes. A dog, birds, leaves, meat going to spoil and get sour. He was the first out on the frontier and gave birth to all of us. There should be a monument to him in Washington, D.C.; instead the New York police had refused him a cabaret card, denied him his livelihood. He hated the black-white split and what was happening to his people, couldn't come up with an answer so he stayed high. Played, fucked, drank, and got high.

76

The way he lived his life he was telling everyone, You don't dig me, you don't dig my people, you don't dig my music, so dig this shit. Didn't answer to nobody but himself, which is the way it should be, 'cause when you go, you go down alone, ain't going to be any friendly little dogs and kids walking along that barbwire fence with you.

In the window of the Flash Record Shop on Western Avenue a few days later there was a black wreath around his last album, and we heard from cats returning from the coast that BIRD LIVES slogans were appearing on the subway walls of New York.

I was on my way to Dick Bok's office to see if I could get a recording contract—he had recorded my first 45 single for Discovery Records in 1952—when Shelly Manne, who had been the drummer on that gig and who I'd done a lot of playing with before the army, stopped me and asked where I was going. When I told him he said, I've got a better idea, there's someone who's anxious to meet you; he drove me to Contemporary Records where I met the president, Lester Koenig. Lester had recorded the Sunday afternoon concerts at the Lighthouse in Hermosa Beach where I played during my unofficial absences from Camp Irwin and had the respect of a lot of people in the industry. He said he'd like to sign me to an exclusive recording contract. I said, Okay but I'm messed up with the union. He asked to what extent, I told him to the tune of three bills and he said to his secretary, Make out a check. Whipped it right on me and that was it. I hadn't had a lump sum like that since my back pay arrived in Yokohama almost two years earlier.

Next day John Bennett, owner of The Haig on Wilshire

Boulevard, phoned and said if I'm available he wanted me to come in with a trio and there was a bass player standing right next to him who would be perfect for me. Things were happening; I wasn't forgotten. I drove down there and the bass player said, I'm Red Mitchell and I think we might have fun playing together. I said, Well let's go in and see. Four bars into "All the Things You Are" I turned to him and said, I think we're going to have fun playing together. With Mel Lewis on drums, and then Chuck Thompson who had played in the Happy Johnson band with me, we began a two-week engagement that stretched to eight months. I can't remember a happier time. It all came together for me during those months— the spiritual harmonies and joyful sound I'd first heard in my father's church with the feeling for time and space I'd picked up from Bird. Red and Chuck grew so close they were breathing with me. Most important we were reaching the audience and I couldn't wait to get to work every night. My hands felt good and my feet were tapping.

We recorded our first album for Lester Koenig one night in June from midnight to dawn at the Los Angeles Police Academy gymnasium in Chavez Ravine. They had a good Steinway there that Artur Rubinstein used, and Lester wanted to get away from the cold studio atmosphere, experiment with a more natural sound. It was a relaxed session, the lights low, Jackie and Red's wife Doe sipping beer at a table behind the piano while we played; on Side 1 I recorded my first ad lib unaccompanied track, the Cole Porter tune "So in Love" which I'd first heard watching a movie in the Big 8 the year of the Iron Mask.

Jackie and I were getting along OK, we still loved each other, but living with her father and stepbrother presented problems. I tried to get her to move to an apartment of our own. We had no chance to be by ourselves. I think deep down the four of us dug one another, there was no great friction to speak of, but nothing belonged to me; I felt like a guest in a boarding house. She was against the move, felt we should be saving money toward a house, but I didn't care about owning a house and didn't want to wait. Maybe I should have pressed her—she might have made the move if she'd thought I was responsible enough to handle it—but I was in no condition at that time to bring about any changes. I sensed our minds beginning to drift apart (one day she suggested I join a golf club—now that would have been funny, me standing around a course with a club in my hand not knowing what the fuck to do), but since I was either high or away on a gig most of the time there was nothing urgent about the drift; it went on quietly, in its own time, like a boat bobbing unattended on calm waters.

From The Haig I took the trio into the Tiffany Club on 8th Street. One night a big, slick, friendly-looking dude came up to me at the bar and said, "I'm Oscar Peterson from Canada, I've been following your work and I like the way you play." I thanked him, said I'd heard his shit and liked the way he played too. We became friends—he took to calling me "Presto," thought I burned like a Presto pressure cooker—and during my breaks I'd go over to Sardi's to hear him play. Between sets at Sardi's one night he introduced me to Billy Shaw, a big-time manager who had booked Bird and now handled Dizzy, Miles, Stan Getz and other heavy people. Shaw said, "I haven't heard you play, but Oscar says I should sign you up. He's never told me that about anyone else so you must be good. I'll listen to your new album when I get back to New York tomorrow. You'll be hearing from me."

A few days later a batch of pages in small type arrived. I called up Oscar and said, What's all this shit? He said, Sign it, he's honest. Early in July Jack Whittemore from Shaw's office phoned and said, Can you leave with the trio for an East Coast trip and open in Cleveland on the 17th? Shit yes, I said. Did we have enough dough to get ourselves there? Shit, no. The bread arrived in the next mail along with a set of directions from Shaw: *Play. Keep your mouth shut. If anyone takes a picture, smile. Leave the rest to me.*

Wardell had taken a gig with Benny Carter's band in Las Vegas, where the big hotels were beginning to integrate— mixing black bands and white audiences. The morning we took off for Cleveland word came from Nevada that he had been thrown from a car and found dead in the desert. A keeper of the flame, one of the first to put it all together. There were times at sessions when he even made Bird turn around and take notice; weren't many who could make Bird do that. Wardell, who couldn't have weighed more than a hundred pounds and wouldn't hurt a flea. Read French philosophers and talked about Henry Wallace. People still ask do I remember Wardell. I was his lieutenant, his kid brother. We never found out what happened in the desert. A few days after the news broke another black wreath was hung in the store window on Western Avenue.

14

On the Road

We came down in Cleveland in one of those old propeller airplanes late afternoon and opened at the Peacock Club that night. As soon as we got ourselves rooms Chuck went down to the ghetto to cop, and that was the last we saw of him till the next day. The club was jammed; Red and I played the first set alone. The owner, a skinny quick-moving cat—looked like he should be dealing blackjack in Carson City—kept pacing around the tables, wringing his hands: "Where's the drummer, where's the drummer." Red and I couldn't very well tell him. Someone tipped us to a cat named Fats Heard who drove a cleaning and dyeing truck and played good. We reached him in a hurry and he finished out the night.

Oscar Peterson was working down the block from us and staying at the same hotel. We'd meet him in the lobby late mornings dressed in his cool-looking casuals, expensive camera around his neck. Have coffee with him, then go our separate ways: Oscar out to the ball park to catch the Indians and Chuck and I down to the ghetto to look for the Man. All week long there were lines outside the club. Our first album, *Hampton Hawes Trio*, had been released to slick reviews and the people were turning out. Though Chuck and I were usually high—Red watching after us, nervous but not showing it—we were disciplined and generally taking care of business, feeling good, stretching out; and when that paycheck came we knew where to go. Next stop the Blue Note in Philly.

In the shadows of the Cleveland airport cocktail lounge I spotted the lady, familiar heft to her, sitting at the end of the bar. I hadn't seen Billie Holiday in almost five years—those early days when she was watching over me, trying to keep me pure and free of sin.

"Hey, Billie."

She looked at me a long time before she said, "You too, baby? I didn't think it would ever happen to you." Probably had heard I was strung but didn't believe it, remembering me as a nice, together twenty-year-old kid playing pretty tunes at Cafe Society.

I said something, asked her where she was headed.

"I thought you were going to get by," she said and the tears came into her eyes.

Still wanting me to escape all that. *But you ought to know, you went through the same garden, went out in the rain and got wet, how was I supposed to stay dry?*

There was nothing I could tell her. A few minutes later she got on a plane to Detroit. It was the last time I ever saw her.

In Philly we kept pulling the crowds. Clifford Brown, the new young trumpet player was in town playing with Max Roach's group that had Bud Powell's kid brother Richie on piano. Clifford was only twenty-three, had learned from Fats Navarro and was coming up fast, burning a lot of people, playing with a big, hungry tone and a flood of fresh ideas. Dizzy, who was still king, had heard him a couple of times and said, That cat's bad. The night before they were to leave for a gig in Detroit, Richie and his wife, who was a slim and beautiful chick, invited Chuck, Red, and me over to the house to have dinner with them. I didn't go. I wanted to wait for the Man to come by and when he came by I overdid it and fell out. The next day Richie and his wife and Clifford set out for Detroit in the rain. Richie's wife was driving. A few miles out of Philly, on the same pike I'd driven down from Cleveland a week earlier, they were wiped out in a crash. I was on the nod; you get numb after a while—so many brothers going down so fast—and all I could think at the time was, Another good cat gone, too bad. We heard that when the news reached London, a musician and close friend of Clifford's smashed every glass on the bar, then picked up a chair and heaved it through the club window.

A few weeks later Benny Golson wrote a pretty tune that Oscar Peterson and other musicians recorded: "I Remember Clifford."

Every so often I'd raise the piano lid on opening night and there'd be a telegram: *Best wishes for a great opening and successful engagement—Oscar Peterson and the Trio . . . Good luck Hampton keep swinging—Oscar.*

The club owners would tell me, Oscar gave a speech about you closing night, told them to be sure and come back next week to hear you. A good brother taking care of his own.

In New York we opened at an east-side club called The Embers. Candlelight and French wine. Sterling silver. Dudes in $300 suits, women in pearls and black dresses, and no one ever stopped talking. From cleaning garbage cans at Lompoc to $1,500 a week at a bourgeois supper club in one short year. Nowhere to go but up.

Slam Stewart and the Chi Chi Girl worked opposite us. After the first set I went over to try out Slam's solovox, which is a small electric keyboard you attach to the piano to get different sounds. "Don't hit that solovox, it don't belong to you," Slam said. I told him I wasn't going to hurt it, I'd never played one before and wanted to see how it sounded. I could tell he was pretty drunk. "I wouldn't let Art Tatum touch that," he said, "and he's the greatest piano player in the world." Somebody behind me said, "No, he ain't, you go on and touch that box if you want." I turned around and there at a front table was the blackest motherfucker I've ever seen. Bamboo-rim shades, carrying a bamboo cane—looked like Jomo Kenyatta or one of those African kings; strong but beautiful. I recognized Thelonious Monk. "Tatum ain't the greatest," he said, "Hamp, come on over." He was with a middle-aged woman who gave off a waft of perfume that smelled like it cost $600 an ounce, and when he introduced me—Baroness Nica Rothschild—I knew I'd guessed right about the price.

The baroness split after a couple of sets, but Monk stayed on. At the end of the night he asked me if I wanted to go to Nica's place for something to eat. I said, Okay, but first I've got to drop by this cat's house nearby to get some music. Don't worry about it, he said, I'll wait. I'm sure he saw through my game. I went into the alley and copped. My man from Harlem had overheard the solovox hassle earlier and asked if I wanted him to get some cats to fuck up the bass player. I said, Shit no, man, he was just a little drunk, but he's a good musician and a nice cat.

Monk drove me in his blue Buick to Nica's hotel penthouse

on Fifth Avenue. When she opened the door I could hear my album playing—the track " 'Round Midnight" that Monk had written. He said to me, "I didn't tell her to put that on." I walked into the room where Bird had died a little over a year ago. A lot of paintings and funny drapes, a chandelier like in an old movie palace, Steinway concert grand in the corner. I thought, This is where you live if you own Grant's Tomb and the Chase Manhattan Bank.

I had heard that when she was younger and living with her family in England her brother turned her on to some jazz records, and when she later moved to Mexico with her husband, a French baron, she'd often split to New York to hear the music and hang out with the musicians. There are other embellishments to the story—her husband breaking her records and threatening to kick her out of the house—but the only important truth is that she loved music and musicians and dedicated her life to them. Her pad became a place to drop in and hang out, any time, for any reason. Monk would fall by, Sonny Rollins with his new record, Horace Silver who wrote "Nica's Dream" for her. She'd give money to anyone who was broke, bring bags of groceries to their families, help them get their cabaret cards, which you needed to work in New York. (If you had a felony conviction or if the police or Alcoholic Beverage Control were even suspicious of you, they would deny you a card. Bird and Billie Holiday couldn't work New York for long periods, and since the major East Coast club work was in town, a lot of people were denied their livelihoods. It was one of those little trips they put on you in those days.) I suppose you would call Nica a patron of the arts, but she was more like a brother to the musicians who lived in New

York or came through. There was no jive about her, and if you were for real you were accepted and were her friend.

This bitch was so rich she had permanent tables reserved at all the clubs and a number you could call from anywhere in New York to get a private cab. If I was sick or fucked up I'd call the number and the cab would come and carry me direct to her pad. On my off nights she'd sometimes pick me up in her Bentley and we'd go around to the clubs. At the Five Spot, listening to John Coltrane's bass player Wilbur Ware solo, if I turned to her and said, "You know what, Nica, Wilbur Ware can *play*," she'd answer in her little clipped British accent, "Oh, yes, he's a motherfucker."

Now and then Monk would drop by the Harlem hotel where Chuck and I were staying (to be closer to the Man), and we'd go drink some orange juice or fall by Nica's. His blackness was so strong, he looked so weird in his variety of shades, canes and hats that people who were fearless and curious would go up to him and start talking. If they asked who he was, he might say, "I got my inside shit and my outside shit, which way you want me to go?" He was ten years older than me, had good sense and understanding—if Wardell was like my older brother, Monk was my father—and never interfered in my life or put me down for being strung. (But the following year, when the shit really got bad, he would be there to reach out a helping hand. If he was using himself, I didn't know it and he didn't show it, and that's what being cool is all about.) We were all brothers on the line, doing our best, each of us trying to find his own way and looking out for each other when we could.

Meanwhile Red, who was staying at a midtown hotel, was keeping an eye on Chuck and me, not letting anyone fuck with us, hating to see us messed up and sometimes sick but, like Monk, with too much soul to cap on us* or try to govern our lives.

It was a wild time, all the cats were there, we were getting fine reviews, people listening to the albums (Lester had released another one) and lining up to hear us. My credentials were finally in order, the apprentice days were over. Miles was running around town in his sharp Mercedes-Benz. Monk and his wife and Nica and I driving down 7th Avenue in the Bentley at three or four in the morning—Monk feeling good, turning round to me to say, "Look at me, man, I got me a black bitch *and* a white bitch"—and Miles pulling alongside in the Mercedes, calling through the window in his little hoarse voice cut down by a throat operation, "Want to race?" Nica nodding, then turning to tell us in her prim British tones: "This time I believe I'm going to beat the motherfucker."

I had found a new connection: skinny, intelligent-appearing cat with glasses, looked like a cross between a sharp doctor and Malcolm X. Tall Man was his name. His old lady made strawberry shortcake every Sunday and dealt pussy and dope on the block; kept the dope in her draws, the only bitch I knew who had two things going for her between her legs, according to your choice. As I was one of Tall Man's special clients he'd hang at the club a lot, and when he couldn't make it he'd leave messages for me: *Tall Man says meet him at the Louisiana Cafe on 125th at 2:30 . . . Tall Man will be at his pad in a half hour. Call.* I was enjoying myself, resigned to being a junkie (if I can feel this fine all the time, fuck it), playing good, people coming to see me; buying a new shirt or suit whenever I wanted and sending $250–$300 home a week

* Put us down.

with plenty left over to cop. Tall Man catering to me, lighting my cigarettes, talkin' about, "Try some of this stuff, Hamp," giving me damn near as much in samples as I was buying. Made me feel important, getting turned on because I was together and on top. It's human nature, anytime you're a winner, you got it.

I was feeling so good I phoned Jackie—she was on her summer vacation—and told her to come on out for the rest of the tour. She said, How can we, it's too expensive. I said, You come along, catch the next plane out. When she arrived I took her to the East Side hotel, where I'd reserved a room, and opened a bottle of champagne. That night Tall Man showed at the club and came over to our table. I introduced him to Jackie as my new road manager (who we will see from time to time). After he left she said to me, "You're a lying motherfucker—he manages something all right, but it isn't roads."

15

You Got Shoes, I Got Shoes

From The Embers we moved crosstown to Basin Street, opposite Ella Fitzgerald. People flattering me, buying me drinks, the young players from the colleges dropping by, making me feel noble and groovy, asking, What's the secret, man, how come the white players don't get it like you? I thought back to the church and the locked piano, all those years strung and tore up, wasting in army dungeons . . . What's the secret. I whipped it on them, putting 'em on easy-like 'cause there's no way of answering that except in a funny way. What I told them was, When I was a kid the white kids whose mamas could afford the lessons were playing Mozart and Chopin and I was at church picking up on "You got shoes, I got shoes, all God's children . . ." then afterward we eat some collard greens, bitches in bedroom slippers cookin' ham hocks in the kitchen hummin' *Mm-hmm,* so when I started playin' naturally it came out "You got shoes, I got shoes . . . mm-hmm" and if you'd been there when you was four you would've ended up playin' the same thing. Shit. There ain't no secret. No two different kinds of music, just *areas* of music. I can play "Someday My Prince Will Come"—dig it,

89

the ofay Disneyland tune—and really groove on it, play the shit out of it 'cause it's a sweet song and the harmonies are so pretty. There's a universal love of that tune by jazz players and that love has got nothing to do with Snow White.

A sucker hits an F chord, it's an F chord. I'll grant you, some suckers hit it cooler than others, but it really ain't no secret. Lots of blacks play blues 'cause they don't know nothin' else. Cat oughta get good experiencing that shit for two hundred years. Just play it, but you've got to love to play, and mean it. Be rich and soulful, brothers. Some people go to school to become doctors and engineers, some make it and some don't. If I tried to play a polka gig those cats would say, Man, you're the squarest, the jivest player in the world. It's a matter of *wanting* to do it. What difference does it make where you go to learn? Toshiko, 8,000 miles from the source, burned the keyboard like Bud Powell (Bud may have used chopsticks once or twice in his life, but I know his eyes didn't slant) and André Watts, black as his namesake, plays Mozart like he's tuned into the grave.

I went through school the best way I could; people trying to make me think I was ignorant and smelled bad. I blamed my education and all the shit that came down on me on my skin; took me a long time to understand I couldn't use being black as a crutch. When I saw Eldridge Cleaver a couple years back clicking his teeth on TV, verbally kicking the Secretary of State's ass, I said, Go on you bad motherfucker, you right, get him. Had respect for him, wanted to say the same thing myself. You got to take pride and stand up, fuck it, we ain't going back to Africa. But coming on militant has to do with right and wrong, not pigment. Today I see a nigger fighting back I say, Damn, stand up for your shit if it's right but don't go out there acting ignorant or expecting favors, talkin' about, Look at my skin.

The thing that messes us up is we're programmed to do this and that; if you want to be educated and civilized you got to be closed up—a secret. When I thought I might want to be a scientist or an artist, Sevener was going to send me to USC. But he scared me, he said, "Well, I'll send you there, but you better make A's," so when the cat in the next block said, Come by my house and we'll play some boogie, that was the way to go, earn my diploma, natural and soulful; get it together, *do it man*. Feel positive. Everything you do is important and connected with everything else whether you're playing piano, harp at St. Peter's gate, or checkers in the park. The way you get up in the morning, smell the leaves, have your juice or something funny like a jelly sandwich and a malt, scratch a dog's head and say hello to some kids, drive your car, go to the can, feel the sun—that's where imagination and soul come from. Having a supply of Laura Scudder's chips in the cupboard that I can come home to makes me feel good. Neighbor of mine once put me on a trip: used to watch me every morning as I got in the car and say, Your right tire's flat. Nothing better to do, standin' out there rakin' the same leaves he'd raked yesterday, tellin' me, Your right tire, I think she's flat. I looked, couldn't see anything; but it affected my driving, my whole day. I'd pull into a station, the attendant would check it out, assure me the tire was cool. But it threw me off, upset my balance.

What's the secret . . . When your ass comes into the world, you're cryin', you ain't no secret. Babies and animals have no secrets. An animal will fuck an animal in the park in front of everybody. I once saw two moths making out—looked good, the one joyful and fluttering, no bigger than my fingernail. A baby boy or girl will pee in your face, cry, turn all red and shake, so you put a diaper on him and hold him, ain't no secret. Reason I can play the blues is I got strung out in the streets and eat collard greens; well, using that kind of basis there might just be some other kind of greens that are *better* for playin' blues. Ain't no secrets about feelin' or cryin' or bein' scared. The only righteous secret is not to *have any* secrets. Everybody got their own shot, their own way to come in.

The labels have been stuck so fast for so many years it's hard tearing 'em away. Lots of ofays still think we all play boogie-woogie and shine shoes, others will tell you you got soul 'cause you've been fucked over. But supposing I hadn't been fucked over, does that mean I have no soul? Some goody two-shoes I've met have more soul than a lot of blacks. Most bourgeois motherfucker that ever showed me some soul was John Kennedy when I was doing ten years in Texas and he reached out a hand to me. (I once had a dream that he'd invited me to a big White House dinner. There were about fifteen forks on one side of the plate and maybe thirteen knives on the other. I had to ask before every course, "Mr. President—never mind the knives—which fork do I use?" and he always answered, straight ahead, "Fifth from the right," or "Third from the left." You know what Nixon would probably answer under the same circumstances? *Let me say this—you have your choice.*)

But I'll tell you, the most prejudiced, jivest, complex, untogether race in the world is blacks. There are so many divisions, so many gradations of color, that's why it's taken us so long to get anywhere; all those years black, brown, high yeller shovin' each other to get closer to the front of the bus. Survival. My best friend married into a light-skinned family and got nervous. If you saw the bitch's father there's no way in the world you'd think he was Negro, that sucker looks like one of them crackers down there in Georgia raisin' persimmons. When my friend's mother-in-law-to-be saw a picture of *his* mother who is darker than him and beautiful, she phoned up to say she didn't think the marriage would be appropriate. *Appropriate* was the word she used. Survival. Mm-hmm.

Jimmy Rushing, the great blues singer who was singing with Count Basie's band when I was doing things to Ann Sheridan in my dreams and reading Batman comics, hired me a couple of years ago to back him on a gig in San Francisco. We were out of different eras, thirty years apart, and he had never heard me play. Was skeptical of me because he knew I'd been born and bred in Southern California. But you know after he heard me take my first chorus of blues he said, "Son, you may o' been brought up in L.A., but you had to have eaten black-eyed peas in Mississippi somewhere along the line." What he was doing was the same thing the ofays did. So those inbred prejudices stick like flies in molasses.

The thing the black cats do, the mistake they make is to try to use their skin to say they're cool. Same as cats strutting out with saxophone straps around their necks to look hip so they can score with chicks, reap the fringe benefits. The time I flew to Albuquerque to meet Jackie I sat beside a sucker in silk vines from Georgia. Feeling a draft, you understand. Chill. Daggers. Probably owned a restaurant where he would've poured syrup down my shirt front and then thrown me out of. A hundred miles out of Phoenix we hit an electrical storm, the plane turned sideways, the stewardess fell down, all the shit fell off the shelves, and people started screaming. The sucker turned and said, "Rough, ain't it?" I said, "You right." He say, "You wanna play some tic-tac-toe?" I say, "I play any damn thing." For that one minute *what happened to Georgia, man? What happened to me, to him?* When the commotion and disturbance had died down a bit he said, "You want me to buy you a drink?" I said, "No, it's cool."

From New York we went to Storyville in Boston, then headed west. Pittsburgh, Buffalo, Rochester, Toronto, Detroit, Chicago . . . In these outlying towns the shit was harder and harder to come by and it became a problem every day to score. The few times I was able to make connections I found people getting burned, turning each other in, reacting to police heat. When my schedule allowed, I flew to New York—those planes weren't setting any speed records in 1956—and when it didn't I'd arrange for Tall Man to fly to me. The second time he came to the hotel in Buffalo Jackie said, "I'm getting tired of this shit, you're really messing yourself up"—then turning to Tall Man, "And you aren't helping matters." Tall Man would say something soothing, "Come on now, you know how it is."

I was no longer enjoying the recognition or the crowds, just waiting for my pay so I could try to cop and keep myself feeling human. In Rochester I made it through most of the two weeks with nothing to sustain me. Got sick, hardly slept—told myself not to panic—and played. Tall Man was hung up in New York. I finally convinced him to risk the mails and he sent me the shit wrapped in a Long Island newspaper. But Chuck couldn't make it anymore and fell out. I called Kenny Burrell who drove up from New York to join us for the rest of the tour. We gave Chuck what money we could and left him sitting on a hospital cot in a white bathrobe.

By the time we reached Detroit Jackie was pretty well fed up. She stayed there with a friend while I went on to Chicago. The police heat was on in Chicago and I knew if I didn't get my ass feeling normal again I'd be joining Chuck in a white bathrobe. On my day off I flew back once more to New York.

Jackie rejoined me in St. Louis. After three days I ran out and knew I was going to get sick again. Bought another plane ticket for New York and was about to make my fourth mercy flight east when Jackie remembered she had a friend in town who was a doctor. He saw I needed help and wrote out a prescription for methadone pills. But for the first time I realized I was in serious trouble and wasn't going to be able to handle it on the road much longer. Getting too hard to rise to the occasion each night. The Shaw office had more gigs lined up after St. Louis which would have taken us back into New York. It was no use; I was tired and sick, tore up. Red and Kenny hated to see me suffer and were ready to call it a day. I cut them loose. Y'all go home. I canceled the rest of the tour and Jackie and I decided to catch a train back to L.A.; I was tired of planes and had never been on a train before. We bought a couple bags of fruit, treated ourselves to a compartment. It was a long, slow trip, and Bird and Wardell will have to rise up out of their graves before I ever do it again.

16

Son, You Hot

I began gigging around town again, using methadone pills when I didn't have the bread to cop. But the pills weren't that easy to come by because the people who were selling them were also selling dope and naturally they preferred that you get strung and go for the higher-priced item. I was beginning to understand that the Man has your destiny in his hands, and if the Man is late for his appointment with you, or doesn't show, you aren't going to be taking care of business. If I had to go to Watts to cop and the cat said, The Man will be here in an hour, and I had to be on the gig in an hour and a half—and the Man didn't get there for two hours—then the arithmetic was simple: I'd be at least a half hour late on the gig. If the Man didn't show, I didn't play. No point in going to work if I was going to be shaking and sweating, throwing up on the bandstand. Keeping my ass feeling normal took precedence; everything else had to wait—music, home, food, sleep.

Sam Sax, a famous West Coast piano teacher who had heard me play at various clubs, called up and invited me to lunch. Said I ought to study with him, that he could teach me to read better and improve my technique and fingering with-

out stymieing my natural talent or quenching my fire. I had
never thought much about fingering; what does it matter which
finger hits what note so long as I'm moving well, my feet are
patting and the shit comes out right? (I've always played by
intuition—the way my hands feel moving horizontally and
falling from black key to white, digging in; if they feel good
my phrasing will be right. One thing that throws me is any
kind of grime on my fingers, or someone else's oil or grime
between me and the board. I've washed my hands ten times in
one night, and if someone has played before me and a towel
is handy I'll wipe the board till it shines. When I was a kid
playing the parlor upright my father told me Paderewski
soaked his hands for a half hour in hot water before playing,
and maybe that's what messed me up. To feel right I need
pure contact with the keys, nothing between them and my
fingers, just as I like to have my hands gripping a clean dry
steering wheel and my fingertips hypersensitive to a woman's
skin; with clean hands I drive better and I fuck better. Sometimes the cleaner you are the funkier you can get; I know the
fresher my hands are the more down and more honest I can
play.) So in spite of the doubts I had, I went out to Sam
Sax's house, not expecting to learn anything but because he
was a nice man and loved music, and I guess I was flattered by
his interest in me.

At lunch he told me of people who were coming to him to
learn how to improvise like me—I'm thinking, Well there're
magazines in doctors' waiting rooms teaching people how to
fuck, fast ejaculation, hot zones, climax and such, maybe you
can teach them how to improvise—and how important I was
in the evolution of jazz, might become a giant in the field one
day. This sweet, sincere cat laying all these goodies on me and

I'm nodding off, my nose in the salad. Afterward we got into a few things, talked about Debussy and Bach and what bad motherfuckers those cats were hundreds of years ago; he wrote out the chords on a tune I'd been wanting to learn, then his daughter, who was also a piano teacher, came in and we played a little together, trading fours.

I never got around to going back. He charged me twelve dollars for the session, three less than his usual fee. His wife told me later he never cashed the check; had it framed instead and tacked it to the wall of his study. I told her it was just as well 'cause I was pretty sure there was nothing like twelve dollars in my account.

By the fall of 1956 I was messing up consistently—showing late on gigs or missing them altogether. Editor of *Down Beat* wanted to reprint some of my album solos in a future issue, would I drop by next week to do the editing? Sure. But at the scheduled time the Man still hadn't arrived and I never got around to *Down Beat*. A Hollywood studio phoned about doing the sound track for a new film. The producers wanted either me or Oscar, and since Oscar was on tour, would I be interested? Wanted to do it, would have paid good, but at the time I didn't even have the bread to get high enough to get to the studio to see what they had in mind.

Though I realized how serious my condition was, I still thought I could beat it. Looking back now, I have to credit Jackie for not turning me in, sticking with me all those years when damn near everybody I brought home was either a dope fiend or a prostitute looking to cop. When musicians were at the house she was often uneasy and would withdraw. She dug only the ones who were taking care of business; Oscar Peterson and Cannonball Adderley were her friends, but Bud Powell could never have got close to her and Bird she would have thrown out of the house. She knew I did what I did because I was sick and couldn't help myself, but I don't think she ever understood how serious the trouble was; maybe no one on the outside really can. She had left the bank and was teaching school by now, making good bread, and if I hadn't been so turned inward, fighting every day to keep myself feeling human, the loyalty and feeling we'd had for each other in the early years might have had a chance to deepen.

I was working with Stan Getz at the Tiffany Club when Art Tatum showed up at the bar one night. Didn't even know he was in the club till he came wandering out of the shadows, moving in that awkward lumbering way, head turned to the side and up—like Bela Lugosi coming at you, scare the shit out of you if you didn't know who it was—straining for light because he only had but a little sight in the one eye. Moved right up to me and said, "Son, you hot. I came down to hear you." Well I knew I was playing good, getting there, but in the overall rundown of players I considered myself comparatively lukewarm at the time. And here's Art Tatum looking weird at me out the corner of one eye, saying, *Son, you hot.* I said, "I'm glad you came and I wish you'd show me some of that stuff you do with your left hand." He said, "I will if you'll show me some of your right-hand stuff. Why don't you come by my house?" Gave me the address and we shook hands on it. *Son, you hot.* From Tatum—that's like the King telling you you're one of the most loyal and courageous subjects in the land. Motherfucker came down to hear me play, shook my hand, said I was hot. It messed up my mind.

I kept meaning to go by his house, but by the time I got my head together and said, Tomorrow I'll go by Art Tatum's house, I heard on the car radio he was dead. Forty-six years old. On November 4, 1956. There should be a federal proclamation for that day—like Labor Day, 'cause he sure must have worked his ass to the bone to play the way he did.

A week later I got together a quartet using Jim Hall on guitar. We recorded twelve tracks in one continuous session from 9 at night to 8:30 the next morning. They were released in three volumes called *All Night Session* and drew some good reviews and a piece in *Time*.

Jack Whittemore phoned from the Shaw office, said he had a couple of weeks for me at the Cafe Bohemia in New York, but I knew I was in no condition to travel east again. I told him I'd better stay close to the pad and hustle.

At the close of the year I won the *Down Beat* Critics' Poll, New Star Division, and was selected Arrival of the Year by *Metronome*. But I was in bad shape.

17

Cattin' with Nica

Fear keeps eating at you more and more every day, you reach the day where you have to stop, look around and think about taking another direction. Any direction but the one you've been heading in.

I had heard about the Public Health Service Hospital in Fort Worth—the western counterpart to Lexington, Kentucky—where you could commit yourself voluntarily. But there were certain formalities you had to observe: Couldn't just walk up to the gate and say, Man, I'm fucked up, let me in. Might be a bum or hobo looking for a place to flop and some warm food. My sister sent for an application blank; I mailed it in and they wrote back, Present yourself at the east gate on such-and-such a date.

I was put in the kick ward which is run dormitory style, like a hospital ward. Methadone three times a day, nurses and orderlies walking by in white coats, TV in the day room, lights out at ten. Wondered why the food looked, smelled and tasted so familiar until I learned that the same dietitians planned for the army and navy. I made friends with a brother orderly who spent his spare time watching the nurses trip by; told me

101

he was willing to let old scores and injustices go unsettled, thought it was time to integrate. I said, You mean you want to stick your dick in some of that white pussy. He said he wouldn't mind some of that. I said, Then you don't want to integrate, you want to penetrate.

After a week and a half I was restless and knew it wasn't going to work. No white psychiatrist was going to be able to help me if he couldn't tell where I was coming from. And how could he, considering his background and mine? A doctor who liked music and had heard of me said, Don't leave yet, you haven't given it a chance. I said, I know but I'm tired of this shit. He said, I wish you'd change your mind, but the key's in your hand. Right, and I'm gonna turn the mother-fucker in the lock, I said, and split.

I caught a bus into Fort Worth, called Jackie and told her to send some money to Western Union so I could get home. She said, I know you're not ready, why are you coming home? I said, Just send the money. She slammed down the phone. I tried one of my sisters: no answer. Phoned Jackie again and said, Will you please send the bread so I can get my ass home. She hung up again. But within two hours the money was at Western Union.

They don't give you any traveling methadone when you leave that fast, and I felt funny on the bus coming back. Jackie was on her way to the beach with a friend when I walked in, and I saw right away she was still drugged. Hadn't expected me for at least three months, probably thinking she was going to see a new man when I got back. Here I was ten weeks early, the same cat. I said, You got the car keys? She threw them on the couch without a word and split. In a min-

ute and a half I was on my way to Watts with but one thing
on my mind: a black eyedropper.

Billy Shaw had died of a heart attack. Some said the
strain of handling Bird and Dinah Washington and all those
fucked-up geniuses had been too much for him. His son
wanted to book me back to the East Coast. I had tried to
straighten out, it hadn't worked, and I was in a restless way,
ready for anything. The itinerary was Pentacoste, New Jersey,
to New York (six weeks at the Composer's Room) to Washington, D.C. I'd go solo and would pick up rhythm players in
New York.

Trying to remember that trip is like asking someone who's
had a 105° fever for a couple of months how he felt, what
went down. If you don't have the same fever when you're remembering, you're likely to miss some details, put a different
slant on others. The ten-week run was a blur of heat and cold,
the harsh or soft lighting in different clubs, Harlem to downtown in a rattling old Buick or shiny Bentley, flash of warm
faces, old friends and brothers from other trips, Monk and
Nica, Miles, Charles Mingus, Sonny Clark . . . Sometimes the
music happened, sometimes it didn't; probably played funny
when I was sick and other nights wouldn't play at all. One
minute be in a Harlem hallway and the next in Nica's penthouse, looking for Monk . . . hear a low, rumbling sound, the
whole place shaking with it and peek through a doorway at a
body layed out on a gold bedspread, mudstained boots sticking out from under a ten-thousand-dollar mink coat and the
body's mouth wide open, sound pouring out of it, and Nica
tiptoeing over, finger to her lips as if I'm about to wake a

three-week-old baby from its afternoon nap, "Shhh, *Thelonious* is asleep."

I closed out in Washington; couldn't pay my hotel bill, left all my clothes in the room and made it back to New York. Fifty cents in my pocket, no clothes and no job, but a thin lifeline stretching to various brothers around town and connections in Harlem.

I ran into Sonny Clark, a young pianist I'd hung with in pre-army days, standing in front of Birdland rubbing his nose. He'd just finished a gig with Dinah Washington and had a hotel room on Central Park West uptown. We decided to split the room rent and cow together.

It was one of those funny little three-story brownstones where show people and musicians stay. Plants in the windows and bare light bulbs in the halls. Big garbage can inside the ground-floor door. Richie Goldberg was there, and Red Garland; and Al Haig, who had played piano on the early Dizzy-Bird records, on a cot in the cellar next to the storage room. Sonny and I began hanging in front of Birdland and the other clubs, hustling brothers for money, collecting from cats who needed to cop, then catching the subway to Harlem. Nights we were short we'd go down to Riverside Records where a friend of ours had a gig sweeping the floors. He'd borrowed so much against his advances they'd put him to work rather than embarrass him, and he usually had enough bread so the three of us could cow.

Central Park West to Birdland to Harlem. I got to know the routes like the tracks on my arms.

Standing under a street light at 45th and Broadway when a brother walks up to me.

"Hamp, what're you doin'?"

"Nothin'." I focus and see it's Charles Mingus.

"Man, I wish you would get yourself together, you got too much talent to go down the drain. I ought to call your father . . . You need some money?"

"Shit, yes."

"I've got a record date for a trio this weekend. You got it if you can get yourself together."

"Would you care to give me a retainer?"

"Damn, Hamp, you won't even spare me."

Now Charles is a strong cat with a temper; on his own trip and unpredictable. There are people who are afraid of him. Been known to lift drums over his head like Atlas holding the world and throw them off the stand 'cause he didn't like the way the cat played. Ever since I first met him in L.A. when I was still in high school, he's always been a perfectionist and dead serious about music—could never stand to see someone not play his instrument right. But there's a gentle and sensitive side to him too. Charles and I came out of the same alley and I'm hip to him.

I fixed and made the date. Sonny came to the studio with me, and though he isn't listed under personnel he played the ending on one of the tracks because I was back in the bathroom fixing again. We got paid after the gig—Charles gave Sonny five dollars for his two chords—and you know we went straight to Harlem and got blind that night.

For the first time in my life I knew what hunger was. I had the dough to buy either food or dope, but never both. Red Garland, who was working with Miles, kept some doughnuts in his room and would give me one from time to time. He was always drawing money from the club so he could get his door unlocked, get back in his room to put on his clothes and go to work. Nice cat, one of the established East Coast musicians who had pulled my coat to the pitfalls of the Apple on my first trip to New York.

Hustling day and night, Sonny and I earned ourselves a righteous moniker: the Gold Dust Twins. Brothers would spot us coming down the street, say, Uh-oh, here come the Gold Dust Twins, and split. We were strung as bad as you can get, way out on the edge and starting to burn people. The only reason we weren't in the park with the muggers was that we were musicians, and I guess something in our natures prevented us from going that way.

Sitting on a bench across from Central Park one afternoon or night, wasted, trying to figure out where my next fix was coming from and what was happening to my life—thinking: from $1,500 a week the year before to sitting on a park bench stone broke with cigarette holes in my pants from nodding, that's a bitch of a drop—when a gleam of sunlight off metal flashes in my eyes and a familiar Bentley rolls up to the curb. Nica behind the wheel and Monk saying, Man, get in this car, a good musician ain't supposed to be sittin' on no bench lookin' like you look.

Back at his place he fed me and told his wife to give me a clean shirt and fill the tub with water. I must have nodded off in the tub 'cause when I came out my skin was wrinkled. Sonny Rollins, who I hadn't seen in over five years, had joined the group. We sat around the little, cramped kitchen, Steinway piled with music next to the refrigerator, and they got right on my case.

"You're an important figure in jazz and you ought to set a better example."

"Okay."

"You got to straighten up and get yourself together before you die or something."

"You right."

"Just 'cause you're stuck out there in L.A., don't think that people out here don't know what you're doing."

"I hear you."

"We heard about you just like you heard about us, we knew there were brothers out there trying to do it. We're all in it together and you're too important to fuck up like this."

"Okay."

Monk took some money out of his wallet, said, Get yourself together and please put something in your stomach too. I accepted it, thinking at the same time, Here's Nica probably worth more than the Chase Manhattan Bank and I've never been able to bring myself to hit on her for bread. I guess you don't like to ask rich people for money if you value their friendship 'cause they might think that's the only reason you're hanging around. Or maybe it was just my pride.

Two nights later I had drifted back to the park bench.

When Sonny Clark and I started bringing back the wrong count to the cats we were copping for I could see danger lurking from the outside as well as the in.

The Gold Dust Twins down and out on Central Park West. Hungry, sick, and tore up. Our room at the hotel was growing so funky when the Man came by he wouldn't do business except out in the hall.

Looked around for one of Sevener's Three G's—grits in the stomach, greenbacks in the pocket, grace in the heart—and when I couldn't even find one, I knew it was time to back up, look at the road sign again.

I phoned Jackie collect and gave her the general picture.

She said to come on home; I told her I wasn't up to robbing a bank and didn't see myself growing wings in the next week or two. She said to stay by the phone; called back ten minutes later and said to call Lester Koenig at Contemporary Records collect. I told Lester the same story and he said, Oscar Peterson's here and he wants to talk to you. Okay. Oscar said, Hampton, the word around is you're in bad shape and maybe you ought to go back to the hospital. Okay, I said, any damn thing, but how do I get out of here? He said, We'll arrange for your admission from here. Call Nesuhi Ertegun at Atlantic Records and he'll get you a plane ticket.

I went by Atlantic Records, got the plane ticket and $50, cashed the ticket that night and went to Harlem with Sonny. Last thing I remember when the money was gone was sitting alone in Nica's Bentley in front of the Cafe Bohemia and Miles poking his head in with his sly grin and asking in his raspy voice, "You cattin' with Nica?" And I'm mumbling, "Yeah, cattin' with Nica," trying to smile with my head on the thousand-dollar wood dashboard.

Nesuhi wouldn't trust me with another ticket and came by the hotel in his Jaguar a day or two later to drive me to the airport. I said to Sonny, I can't handle it anymore, man, I'm going back down to Fort Worth. He said, Well, I hope you get your shit together. I said, You too, and shook his hand. It was the last time I saw him alive.

Back up to kick ward, knew my way cold by now, rubbin' my nose, wondering what I'd done with my sunglasses. (Sonny's room, Monk's pad, glove compartment in the Bentley?) Made it through three weeks this time—letter came from *Playboy* forwarded by Jackie, my All-Star Jazz Poll certificate of merit—but I was too far gone; it's just too hard lying there suffering when there's no one sitting on you to make you stay. Unlocked the door to the outside again and in one of those quick looks into the future which you try to shut off because it's clouded with pain, I realized I was probably going to have to get locked up and the key stashed out of reach in order to really get it together.

18

B-29

I think I knew something was funny all along but I couldn't pinpoint it. Little coincidences that would pull my coat . . . people smiling too bright, someone following me, turning into a drugstore when I stopped to look. Clues that should have warned me to stay cool. But my energies were so focused on getting fixed that I hadn't the time to do anything but mull these things over for a minute, then they would be gone from my mind.

It was the summer of 1958. I was working at Sherry's with a drummer and a bass player I'll call Wally Shade. The standard sort of club on the Strip: street people, college kids, a few gangsters who liked the music.

Everyone on the street was hip to Wally; knew he was a heavy user who had got busted but had never done time. They knew he might still be on the payroll—the police would put bounties on us, like going hunting, Wally was a bounty hunter —and since no one else would supply him he was forced to come to me. Now my strategy was to put Wally to my own use: buy for him from my connection and use some of the proceeds to buy for myself. Since he was strung and no one else would fool with him, he'd naturally have to protect his only source—me. But I made sure he always shot up in front of me, consumed all the evidence, so when he left the premises he was clean. Outslicking him and the cops all down the line, you dig. It was a risky game, and for a while it went my way.

About a month after this arrangement with Wally had been in effect, a Mexican cat I'll call Vince started dropping by the club nights. Young and clean-cut, something old-fashioned about him; looked like a bellboy in one of those W. C. Fields one-reelers. Liked the music, would request tunes off my albums, buy me a drink. Said he wished he could be a musician. I said, Go ahead, all you gotta do is keep your instrument clean and pat your feet right.

One night he said to me, if I were you I'd be careful of Wally Shade. I said, I'm hip to Wally, it's cool.

A few nights later he came in during intermission and said, Your bass player's down the street talking to a state agent. I said, You sure? He said, Come on, I'll show you. We drove past the corner and saw Wally talking to a cat leaning against a light-colored Fairlane Ford: another Terry and the Pirates type, crewcut in a brown suit and funny tie. I said to my Mexican friend, You know something? I think you right.

Naturally I didn't let on to Wally that I knew; that way I could stay a step ahead of him. It was just another little lug dropping, telling me to be cool. Strung as I was, I figured I was still at least an inch ahead in this game. I wasn't prepared for the cloak and dagger shit that followed.

It wasn't long before Vince was asking about dope, said he had a couple of whores who were having a hard time keeping straight. I suppose I should have been more suspicious, I knew he was lying, but when you're strung you're greedy, and when you're greedy you're not going to be taking time to analyze motives. I said, If you're serious why don't you give me a call.

We closed out at Sherry's and a little while later Vince called me. I bought $300 worth for him, making sure I took out my taste. The second time he bought he came to the house for the stuff. Jackie and her father were out, a couple of other cats were there and we were fixing. I was shaking my arm, swinging it around like you do to make the blood come up, and Vince said, "Wow, looks like a B-29." One little corner of my head told me, That's a funny expression to use, something's happening here, but another corner said, If it *is* happening, it's too late, nothing you can do about it; might as well tie up, get that last drop before the dam breaks—bust me tomorrow, but let me be high today.

The next time, a month later, Vince called and said he would drop by the house again if it was all right. I said I had some people with me, it would be cooler if we met on the corner.

When Vince drove up there were two cats in the back seat. Again my instinct told me what was happening, but that other corner of my head said, Go on, everything's cool; doesn't make any difference 'cause if it's the Man they got you anyway, if it isn't you're straight. I got in the front seat, turned around to greet the cats in back, and Vince put a .38 caliber pistol to my head. For a second I thought, He's hip to the wrong counts I gave him the last two times (mixing in the baking soda) and is going to shoot me down like a dog. Well, live fucked up, die fucked up, I'm thinking, when Vince flashes a little gold badge alongside the pistol and says, Hampton, you're apprehended. Federal agent. I said to myself, Ain't this a bitch. Outslicked by a Mexican, a nigger, and Terry and the Pirates.

When they busted me I had 16 cents in my pocket: November 13, 1958, my thirtieth birthday. Snatched out of the ballgame in the prime of my life. Jackie had baked a pineapple cake with coconut frosting for the occasion. I never got to taste it.

Instead of taking me downtown they brought me to Glendale and booked me under a false name (looked at a Compton Street sign on the way and I became George Compton). That's a standard number they do in order to jam* you; figuring to turn me into a bounty hunter like Wally Shade. I said, Shit, no. They said, As of now there's no record of your arrest, George. You can do twenty years, sit here and think about it a minute. But then, as people with no brains or soul will sometimes do, they proceeded to fuck up on their chain of command, and when the shift changed that night the new cat, unaware of what was going down, said, Have they taken your picture and fingerprints yet? I said, No, better go ahead and take 'em, bring all the shit up to date.

They came around the next morning and said, You done any more thinking? I said, Motherfuckers, you booked me falsely. They said, You're dreaming, you have no record. I said, My dream's come true. Go look in the file under Hawes.

That afternoon they took me into L.A. and booked me properly.

I wasn't in the county jail but one night, sleeping on a cold cement floor—it was so crowded they were putting one more cat in each cell than there were bunks, last one in gets the floor—when I got sick and they took me upstairs to some little jive room that served as an infirmary. But they didn't know

* Coerce into becoming a police informer.

what they were doing up there; I just had to lay in bed and kick cold.

I never heard what happened to Wally Shade. Since he had blown his cover for good I wouldn't be surprised if he'd gone to jail the same time I did. When a bounty hunter burns out he will eventually have to serve his time.

19

Five Christmases

There were so many good people who got busted in that decade between '55 and '65 that didn't deserve it. Friends of mine who were caught in the same dragnet as me and tried to fight it got twenty years. They should have known better because those of our generation who were using and rebelling were getting slammed down hard and the word going around was, It's no use, be cool.

Just before sentencing I was visited by a fine, light-skinned black bitch who asked me how I'd like to pay these white motherfuckers back. I said to her, You work for the blue-eyed man, don't you. She gave me a funny look and split. Next day I pleaded guilty and got a dime.*

I think Jackie still believed I'd only be going to the hospital again—maybe a year for using and come out cured—until that judge said, Ten years. Two mornings later they shot me back before another judge to testify against a supplier in a different case they thought I might be connected with. Offered me immunity. I said to the judge, You can't give me immunity, I just got ten years for the same shit. Should have stopped there

* Ten years.

but I kept on—You people have had me under your thumbs tryin' to make me tremble, sendin' me out in the street to hunt down friends. Well you can put me in a dungeon and I'll turn into a motherfucking prune, but you won't break me. Fuck you and the Treasury Department and the FBI—

Jackie stood up, shaking. *Hampton, what're you doing?*

Fuck you too, I said.

The judge said, Two years to run concurrently.

The marshal who took me back to the county jail said, You're a stupid son of a bitch, but I'll say one thing, you got a lotta heart.

In the narcotics tank all the federal prisoners had red slips stamped U.S. All the others were state prisoners. Anybody who had a red slip was a bad cat—everyone else looked up to him because he had to have done something far out for the government to bust him; it was a badge of recognition.

On a summer day in 1959 after I'd been locked up for seven months a deputy ordered about ten of us red-slip people to roll 'em up—by which he meant roll up your mattresses and collect your personal belongings. Gonna be some changes made, new scene. Okay, had to be better than this. Only good things I remembered in seven months were the variety of little pies a cat named Oscar brought around that only cost you a dime. We were herded out the back door of the hall of justice, across to the federal building and upstairs to the marshal's office. At the same time streams of other cats from different tanks were all converging on the Federal Building; it was like a mass exodus except there wasn't going to be any Moses leading us out of L.A. In the marshal's office a platoon of feds who must have mistaken us for Georgia lepers came at us with arm and leg chains. Our hands and legs were cuffed, one leg chained to someone's else, then groups of us were marched to the elevator clanking like Christmas ghosts.

It was in the elevator that I had my final contact with a young chick. We were all jammed inside ready for the descent when the door opened again and two county women sheriffs squeezed in with three fine bitches. They were handcuffed but unchained 'cause never in a hundred years could you mistake any one of these bitches for a Georgia leper. I asked the one standing in front of me as we descended how she'd been busted and she told me she'd been getting twenty-six allotment checks from twenty-six servicemen she was married to. Her hair had a jasmine smell, she was so fine I said to her, "Baby, I wish they'd take these chains off and let me fuck you quick because you in big trouble and so am I." She said, "Well, I can't do that, but I'll back into you." And went ahead and did it, backed her ass right into me and kept it there. Everybody in the car fell out. When the women sheriffs finally pulled us apart I called to her, "Beautiful, maybe that'll hold me for a minute."

Our destination was Fort Worth which was becoming like a second home to me. The train ride took three days. You slept in a bunk with the cat you were chained to and if he had to go to the can you went with him, standing outside with the chain stuck in the door. Most of the first-offense cats were nervous and had a right to be. I tried to set their minds at ease. The atmosphere's going to change, I told them, you'll be more like a patient than a prisoner. They couldn't believe it. No guards, no guns? No armed guards, I said, only thing is your ass is going to be lodged in one continuous tunnel.

The first inmate I saw at Fort Worth was Stymie. I'd met him the last time I was there. He had been one of the "Our

Gang" kids, a famous black child actor when there was hardly
any such thing, but nobody has heard of him for a long time.
Now he was houseboy to the head doctor, pretty much free to
come and go, with access to different departments. No one is
supposed to talk to the incoming inmates until they're released
into the general population, but Stymie came busting into the
medical room where I was waiting for my exam and said,
"Hamp, how you doin'? Was it a dime?" I said, "Yeah, it was
a dime," and he said, "Well, that was the wire we got." (The
grapevine has always been strong in these joints because the
same junkies are constantly being shifted around and filtered
through the different prisons and hospitals.)

After the physical I was taken straight to the kick ward
where the people coming off the streets are held until they're
considered clean enough to be turned out into the population.
Now having been incarcerated in an L.A. tank for seven
months I sure as hell was clean, they could see that, but they
started reviewing my records, which by that time had blos-
somed into a pretty far-out dossier (probably had my army
files, all those weird trips) and decided the time wasn't quite
ripe for me to be turned out. I was kept in the kick ward for a
month on hold. Stymie said he thought they were considering
putting me in the nut ward of the hospital or sending me to
McNeil Island, which is hardcore and maximum security.

The doctor they sent to interview me looked over the
records and said, "You sure have done a lot of crazy things,
Hampton." I told him that at the time I did them it didn't seem
to make any difference whether I did them or not. He said,
"Would you like to stay at Fort Worth?" and I said, What
difference does it make, neither me or any of my people are

getting shit. I'm locked up, got to stay somewhere, here or outside chained to a tree.

A few days after the interview I was released into the population and assigned to a regular ward. Probably decided this cat's so messed up, been strung out so long, we better keep him here for psychiatric treatment; if he gets too funny we can always ship him out. What they were doing then was leaving it up to me, which was the best thing they could have done.

In an innocent, ungreedy kind of way those doctors were like the jackleg preachers, all robes and ceremony. It wasn't that any of them were dumb or incompetent, but if you start with someone like me who has come out of the haven of the church into the streets, playing jazz and messing with dope, why there's no white psychiatrist in the wide world qualified to analyze me because wherever he would start from, whatever funny little program he tried to work me into, his thinking is going to be alien and wrong. He's going to go into his generalizing bag, and that's the big mistake down front because there is no way he can possibly conceive of where I'm coming from. So it isn't their fault that most of the time they don't know what they're doing.

The first night I was assigned to a ward I could feel the buzzing and electricity through the dining room. The word had filtered through that Hampton Hawes was down from kick ward, and I guess it was inevitable there was going to be a session that night. I hadn't played piano in over seven months. When I walked into the band room after dinner it seemed like every cat in the hospital had a pass, looked like a therapy room the way they were jammed in, sitting on top of the piano, spilling out into the tunnels. Bass and drums set up, a couple of horns. We left the doors open and started playing, drawing in some of the doctors and nurses who dug it and a few funny Texas guards who didn't know what to make of the music, wondering what the hell's going on, what are all these people doing down here? Well we cooked pretty good, no one trying to shoot anyone else down, no peacock feathers in view, just easy blowing on old standards and one cat sitting atop the piano, feet dangling in my face, calling down, "I heard about you before, you a bad motherfucker." Came nine o'clock when the band room was supposed to close, we played right on through and every now and then some old Texas cracker guard would poke his face in, saying, "What are all these people doin' in here after hours?" He had no idea what was going down; heard the music, but it didn't register, *weird* seeing all these people jampacked in, hardly a breath of air in the room. What the hell's goin' on? Probably thinking, They're shootin' craps or something, big dice game, crazy junkies.

On July 4th I wrote to the Attorney General, told him a dime was a long time for what I did, the days were moving slow, and would he send me some information about how I could get out before 1969. His office wrote back a polite letter saying, Man, don't bother us.

A week later I read in the paper that Billie Holiday had died in New York, her deathbed a hospital cot guarded by city police. They had hounded her right up to the last day. But I knew she would live on, that she had just said Bye for a while.

My first gig was mopping the tunnels with 11 other cats from 10 P.M. to 4 A.M. with a half-hour break for "lunch"— not knowing what else to call it at two in the morning. When I didn't fuck up and they saw I was cool they gave me a day gig in the band room issuing instruments and taking inventory. Had a chair and desk, access to a Steinway spinet. But every time I started to play, cats would drop in to listen, so I had to stop. I wasn't in a performing mood, just wanted to play some shit for myself. My assistant was a big dude with a shiny bald head and bushy beard, looked like Man Mountain Dean. Wore gold hoop earrings and said to me one day, Watts, I have a problem. (Various cats would call me that, knowing I was from L.A.) I said, I'm no psychiatrist, but what's your problem? He said, I think I'm a homosexual. I said, All highways got at least two lanes, and as long as everybody isn't driving on the same one there won't be any crashes. He said, What're you trying to tell me, Watts? I said, I wouldn't be interested in that trip myself, but if that's your pleasure, pursue it.

I fell into the routine: vocational therapy and all the other funny little programs. Little by little I could feel my suspicions and fears of the hospital and the people who ran it slipping away. Some of them understood I shouldn't have been there, not for ten years anyway, and were sympathetic. By letting me know they felt for me and wanted to help, they made me want to try. Probably the most sensible thing you can do for someone in a situation like mine is to forget the psychiatrist-patient relation—our worlds are too far apart, it's like Jupiter trying to do something for Mars—and just be nice to him, allow him his dignity, provide the facilities and let him work out his own shit in his own way.

But I couldn't help looking at the calendar from time to time. October 1959, January 1960 . . . Release Date was 1969, well past my prime. Be hard getting back in the ballgame when you're over forty. I kept feeling in my pocket, but there was no key there.

Just after my second Christmas in the joint Jackie wrote that Sam Sax had died after a long sickness. She said that near the end he had asked her to send me a message: "Tell Hamp he's the greatest, and I'm going off to play a jam session with the angels."

Jackie came to visit me once a year. The second time she asked me, What should I do? I said, The best thing to do is cut me loose; no need for you to suffer just 'cause I got my black ass busted. She let me know she had another man but didn't want to divorce me. I told her I didn't want her using my name if she was fucking someone else. She said she was sorry, she couldn't help it.

The hardest time to pull was at night when I thought about Jackie and home. I dealt with it by reading and drawing; some of my pictures might still be hanging on the ward walls.

The only other member of the family to come by was my sister Edith. She was on a trip with her husband and took a fifty-mile detour to see me, which was nice. I remembered how fat she was as a kid and how I used to make fun of her. If you're drugged take it out on your fat sister, right? She went back and told the others I was okay. I guess they were embarrassed; first member of the family to offend society and go to jail; the youngest, most talented, and the black sheep.

One day someone called down to Dr. Kay's house where I was working as houseboy and said, Send Hawes up to the auditorium. The Ringling Brothers Circus had come to put on a show and their piano player had got lost. As the patients were filing in I asked the manager what he wanted me to play; he said, Background music, anything you want. Show opened with a fire-eater. I tried to remember what the soundtrack had been like in the old Burt Lancaster movies when the cat swallows the flaming sword and wove in some of those side-show sounds. Next came some chicks and a clown followed by animal acts, funny little dogs in skirts and sweaters. I'd play something appropriate when I could think of it and lay out when I couldn't. (Glad there weren't any elephants, that would have stumped me.) The last act was three chimpanzees dressed in gingham suits on roller skates. I was running out of ideas so I went into some medium tempo blues. Those chimps kept skating round and round the piano. One of them shot by pretty close, I looked into the motherfucker's eyes and he gave me a funny look right back as if he was thinking, "Man, what you playin'?" Probably having trouble coordinating his moves with the beat. When it was over the manager said I had done fine and if I needed a gig when I got out to give him a ring. I thought, Damn, I'm more versatile than I thought I was.

Just after my third Christmas I was watching John Kennedy accept the Presidency on the Washington steps. Something about the look of him, the voice and eyes, way he stood bright and coatless and proud in that cold air . . . I thought, That's the right cat; looks like he got some soul and might listen.

The next day I told one of the medical officers I wanted to apply for a Presidential pardon. He said, That's the root of your trouble, Hampton, you refuse to be realistic. When you leave here you're probably going to go back to dope because you'll still be thinking unrealistic. As I said before it wasn't basically their fault that those doctors' heads were all fucked up.

They put so many obstacles in my path—warning me the effort would be useless and I'd be worse off than before—that it was a year before I even found out the name of the pardon attorney I had to contact. Meanwhile I took care of business, played some piano, watched the volunteers come in on their three-to-six-month commitments, go back out on the streets and be back in the tunnels a week, month, or year later.

Late in 1962 the official form finally arrived: Application for Executive Clemency. Raft of pages in funny type and at the bottom of the first page the date 1923, so I knew nothing in this field had changed for a long while.

Most of the brief was made up of routine information questions. The last page was the heavy one—the place where you explained your reasons. I decided I didn't want to make it a personal cry for help. What I did was send John Kennedy a directive: As you are the Commander-in-Chief it is my duty as a citizen to inform you that an injustice has been perpetrated, one of your people is being subjected to cruel and unjust punishment, and it is your duty to consider the evidence and reciprocate. Made it professional and detached. I wasn't asking for a shoulder to cry on. It was as if I were an officer in battle informing my commander that as things are coming down at present we're getting our ass kicked, might be a good idea to switch to plan B. And then to round it off I added some heavy legal shit in Latin I'd dug up in the library.

Now at the time I was in the honor ward. Established, nonfretting. Cool, docile, and not contemplating escape. Had my own room, unlimited TV privileges, first in chow line, free to walk on the grounds; it was the next thing to the streets. I'd made a lot of friends among the staff and started collecting letters of recommendation to go with the brief. I hadn't won anyone over, no one thought it was any use, thought I was crazy to try, but they wanted to help me take my best shot.

On the afternoon of my fourth Christmas they showed a

movie, "The Alamo." There was a sweet tune on the sound track, "The Green Leaves of Summer," that kept humming through my mind and I told myself I would try to record it if I ever saw daylight again.

In January of 1963 news came through the grapevine that Sonny Clark had OD'd in New York.

By March I had collected eighteen letters of recommendation and made my move: sent the letters with the application to the President and tried to forget about it.

In April I wrote my first letter home to my mother and father . . . *I don't blame you or anyone else for what's happened, you were trying to help. You took a direction you thought was cool so don't dwell on any mistakes, rid your conscience of all that stuff, it's all right, I love you.* Sevener wrote back, You know, your mama had a heart attack a while ago but she's feeling better now.

In May I heard on the grapevine that Bud Powell was down, out, and fucked up in Paris.

In July I was let out for an afternoon to play a jazz concert at Texas Christian University. My first day on the outside in five Christmases. Later one of the musicians said he'd heard Ladybird Johnson was in the audience and that was probably how it all came about. But I was looking inward and didn't see any ladybird there that day or any other kind of bird.

On August 16, 1963, the President of the United States came through.

I woke up in the morning just as I'd been doing for five years, took my little funny case into the can to wash up and brush my teeth, headed for chow as usual, here's another day, man, and was stopped by a security guard. Deputy MOC wants you at the administration building. The guard drove me over.

Doctor Foley, the deputy medical officer, said, "Good morning, Hampton." Cool. Behind his desk were two flags, the American flag and the public health service flag, and between them a big color picture of John F. Kennedy. "I've got some news for you, Hampton." He turned and called through a doorway to another doctor and now his voice was shaking a little—"Would you come in Bob? I want you to hear this." He showed Bob the paper. "Ever see one of these?" Bob's eyes got wide and he shook his head. "Never." So the two top cats in the hospital told me to my face that my struggle was over, the long five years was over and I wouldn't have to do the other five. Executive clemency granted by authority of the President of the United States. I had my final diploma.

I sat down and asked them to read it again.

That's it then, I said.

Yeah, they said and handed it to me. Saw a blur of Gothic letters on parchment paper, about twenty "whereases," signed with the Man's name.

I said when can I leave.

They said forthwith.

By the time I got back to the chow hall the grapevine was already alive, Stymie whipping it on everyone and the word spreading like flash fire. Nine hundred cats in there eating breakfast and most of them seemed to be jumping up against the rules, crowding around to shake my hand, bewildered and happy—those that liked me happy and the others bewildered. I moved through it all wooden, like a dead limb, hardly re-acting to any of it 'cause you can't immediately react to something that heavy. We were moving through the tunnels—

chaplain saw me, took a little jump in the air and yelled "Hallelujah!"—aids, security guards, nurses crying, a lot of well-wishers tagging along, all those cats I wasn't going to see any more, taking me to some building to be processed out; records put in order, personal stuff gathered, bags packed, put him in a suit and tie, make a plane reservation.

I haven't shaved yet, I said, dazed.

Hasn't shaved yet! Man's sprung him and the crazy mother-fucker wants to shave.

Someone drove me to Dr. Kay's house on the edge of the grounds. Don't know what I was doing there, but I was up-stairs shaving in his pink-tiled bathroom, going through the motions looking at myself quiet and stone dumb in the mirror, when his wife busted in so glad and excited she practically jumped on my back, hugging me then backing off and looking at me with shaving cream on her face and tears in her eyes. And the doctor calling up to get my ass downstairs 'cause we had to get to the airport.

Next thing I remember I was drinking a toast with his family downstairs, and now the curtains were parting a bit, clear light showing through, and it began to come in on me what had happened. August, Texas, dig it. Hot as blazes in the little linoleum kitchen. My first drink in five years. Made it. President told them to let me go. Right? Laid it on him in Latin. Some hope left in the world. Nine years strung out, all those hospitals and dungeons, right? Made it, kicked. Standing up with this fine family, tall, straight, not fucked up. Looking good, feeling strong . . . together . . . confident. Never been so confident before. And all these people who'd helped me thinking a miracle had happened. Wasn't no miracle. The only thing that had happened was the most ordinary thing in the world—somebody was watching over the country. President sitting up there in his tower and a small cry for help had come out of the dungeon, filtered on up there. And the powers that be answered back, you don't need to feel alone anymore. Wasn't no miracle. What happened was normal, the kind of thing that's *supposed* to happen if the person on the throne is watching the shop, doing his job. So how could it be a miracle?

American Airlines lifting over Fort Worth. Heading west, thirty thousand feet over the Pecos River. Dig it. Cute little smiling stewardess in an orange cap coming in at me with the first words I'd heard on the outside in five years. "Good afternoon, sir, would you like coffee or a beverage?" I said, "Baby, please bring me a hard drink, any kind at all." And when she returned with it, still smiling, the cute little cap perched just so on top of her hair, she said, "How was your day today?" Like I was coming back from a week's vacation on a dude ranch or visiting my old grandmammy in Abilene. How was your day today. "Just beautiful," I said.

20

Autumn Leaves Turning Blue

She had recovered and was home from the hospital. When we walked in the door she ran to me, crying and kissing me, "Here's my son, my son's come home . . ." The sudden change scared me, I'd never seen her let go like that. She held me for a long time, her tears washing my face, and I thought, Imagine going through all the shit she's been through, the years of feeding and keeping us warm, always there, holding her emotions in check, and still have love and sweetness in her heart.

My immediate aim was to make up for the time I'd lost, reestablish my credits, and convince people I was responsible and no longer strung. There were those who couldn't believe I was clean and probably never will; others were uneasy, wanting to make sure.

It's hard building back up what you tore down. People in L.A. still remembered me because most of my action had been there, but in Chicago, New York and other outlying cities I was forgotten. A lot of young musicians had come up while I was away. When you're off the scene for five years you may as well be dead.

I carried a letter from my probation officer in case I got stopped in the street at night: letting the police know I had government permission to pursue my career. So don't fuck with him too much, he's paid up and looking for work.

Did five years for an apple, ate the motherfucker and didn't look back.

Monk was in town, working the It Club on Washington Boulevard. I hadn't seen him since 1957 when he'd given me a clean shirt, a bath, and a pep talk at his pad in New York. I caught him at the bar between sets; he didn't seem to recognize me. Looked over my shoulder, his elbow on the bar, staring into space the way he sometimes does. Now five years in a tunnel is bound to change you, but I didn't think I'd changed that much. I said, "Monk, it's me, Hampton." He kept staring past my shoulder as if he hadn't heard, then turned his back and went into a little shuffling dance; danced a couple of quick circles around me, danced right up to me and said, "Your sunglasses is at my New York pad." And danced away. It was his funny way of telling me that someone on the outside had been thinking about me.

Bill Sampson, owner of Mr. Konton's on Sunset, phoned and said he wanted me to play my first gig at his club starting in a week. I told him I'd had another offer and he said it would be worth a hundred dollars to him if I would turn it down. Okay. Never been paid *not* to work before. We pulled a good opening-night crowd, a lot of old friends and some movie people, and I thought, Shit, I might not have to contact Ringling Brothers after all. Miles came to town a few days later. He dropped by, threw his arms around me and said in his husky voice, Did they make a faggot out of you? I said, No, but I learned how to mop and cook. It was a groovy and relaxed eight weeks, a nice welcome home. *Down Beat* gave me a good review, said my prowess was unaffected by the long absence, and on a rendition of "Falling Leaves" *he painted a tonal picture, slipping in sly and brilliant runs and figures until the autumn leaves turned blue.* Far out. Never been able to pull that off before.

The same day that a letter came from a friend at Fort Worth saying that six hundred cats had applied for Presidential pardon after I left, there was a picture in the L.A. paper of the judge who had sentenced me to ten years. Dead of a heart attack. I thought back to the CO at Camp Irwin in Barstow who had court-martialed me and sent me out to the Mojave Desert to sizzle for three days—had *his* ass canceled in similar circumstances—and wondered if that weird patron saint of strung-out musicians wasn't still watching over me, taking revenge in his peculiar way.

Not long after that I appeared on Steve Allen's TV show and *Sepia* came out with a five-page spread: *Profile of a Jazz Giant . . . the slender (five-foot nine-inch, 156-pound) son of a retired Los Angeles Presbyterian minister who frankly admits to a certain amount of personal introvertedness . . . dresses immaculately, lives in a modest, but neat, well-furnished and sparkingly-clean, East Side Los Angeles home with a loyal and adoring school-teacher wife, Jacqueline, who laments the fact that Hamp's spiraling career leaves them too little time together ("I'd love to be in his arms all the time.")* . . . which gives you an idea of the general tone of the piece. My probation officer had caught the Steve Allen show, said he was proud of me and was going to write to Ed Sullivan to get me on that show. He sent the letter to Sullivan in an official government envelope. When he didn't get an answer he was drugged and bewildered, couldn't understand it. I told him not to worry about it, what had probably happened was that Sullivan had taken a look at the envelope, figured the income tax people were after him, and threw the motherfucker out unopened.

I wanted to record right away but Lester Koenig said to cool it and relax, get used to my freedom and working again. I had been thinking more about the Dmitri Tiomkin tune I'd heard on "The Alamo" soundtrack that last Christmas day; it had the same sad and lonely feeling he'd worked into "The Ballad of High Noon," and variations had been growing in my mind. When Lester finally set up a date I decided to record it as a jazz waltz with an extended ad-lib solo introduction. The album came out a few months later under the same name as the title tune, "The Green Leaves of Summer," and got a good reception. (One track was an original dedicated to Dr. Kay at Fort Worth; it was a straight-ahead improvised blues, not the kind of tune you'd come out of a record shop humming, and I hope he wasn't too disappointed.) The jacket photo shows me trim and cleancut and it was a pretty accurate reflection of where my head was at in those days. It felt good to be looking right and thinking right instead of sitting in a park in scroungy clothes like a bum worrying about the police and trying to figure out where my next fix was coming from. Felt ten years younger. I was no longer using, the craziness was dampened down; had my little ritual before leaving the house to go to work: shine my shoes, put on the funny suit and tie, check the handkerchief, match up the socks. Coming on sober, nonfeverish and respectful, you understand, after some fifteen years at 102-105 degrees. Looking back on that photo now, ten years later, I might have been the Super Fly of 1963, the Flash Gordon of the niggers.

In the autumn of my first year out—three months after throwing me the lifeline that reached from the White House to Watts—John Kennedy was murdered in Texas.

21

Swimming Pool

On my way to play a gig in Vancouver with Harold Land I stopped at the federal building in Seattle to pick up my permit to leave the country. (Since I was still on Conditional Release I had to let them know where I was going, what I'd be doing when I got there and how long I'd be doing it.) That same day LBJ was due in town to campaign against Goldwater. The downtown streets were blocked off, bunting strung from telephone poles and street lamps; when I came into the area a motorcade was already forming, flags flying. Big day in Seattle. I didn't pay it much mind, I couldn't vote anyway. Took the elevator up to the fifth floor, saw a number on the door that seemed to match the one on the lobby directory and walked in on three hefty middle-aged black women carrying shopping bags and dressed in funny old-time dresses and scuffed shoes, one of them with an Aunt Jemima bandanna around her head. The kind of sisters you'd see any day of the week in Harlem or Watts, working in Mel's Kitchen or out buying the old man's supper. Except that the one with the bandanna was fitting a submachine gun into her bag and was looking at me with a pair of small, cold, mistrusting eyes. Naturally I split. Took the elevator back down to the lobby to recheck the directory, thinking what a slick ruse that was because anybody wishing harm on LBJ would be on the watch for some ofay blond lieutenants mingling with the crowd, cats in laundered dungarees and poplin jackets. Sure wouldn't be suspecting three Aunt Jemimas with big old black asses looking like they just come out of the grocery with greens and hambones stuffed in their bags. Shit no. President was in good hands. They'd learned their lesson last November.

In the spring Jackie and I and her father moved to another house in Compton, a town just south of Watts. I wanted more than ever to get a pad of our own so we could run our own lives, but her head was still in that other camp: Why go to that expense when we could keep on renting from her father and save money? I suppose I should have pressed her, told her I was going and if she wanted to hang with me, solid; if not, Bye. But then I'd remember how she had layed dead* all those years I was at the hospital and figured I owed her some kind of gratitude for going through those changes and not abandoning me.

The Compton house was big: four bedrooms, fireplace and intercom, two-car garage, a yard and swimming pool. I wasn't unhappy to be leaving the east side. The police had been jacking people up** there, I knew my turn would come sooner or later and there was no way I was going back to jail; they'd have to shoot me down in the street. The past five years I'd got in the habit of having my life ordered and I went along with whatever Jackie wanted, let her run the show just as she had

* Stuck by me.
** Harassing.

during those early years when I was strung and not too aware of the day-to-day realities. Some brothers who dropped over felt funny in the house. Not many cats who play jazz got a fireplace in a bedroom and a pool, they said. But I couldn't take pride in any of it; there seemed to be no life or warmth in the rooms.

After the excitement of being free had worn off—the big splash I thought I'd made on my return, the reception at Mr. Konton's, appearance on national TV, good reviews on my new album—the truth began to sink in: I wasn't doing all that good, and things didn't look too bright up ahead. I was thirty-seven years old, big house and car, all the clothes I wanted, food in the icebox, money in my pocket but I had no incentive to do anything, no discipline, no momentum. Willing to just let things happen, like a dead leaf on a tree ready to fall. All those goodies had somehow tipped the balance too far to one side. Might as well be living in a tent or an igloo, eating blubber. It was going to be a tougher road back than I thought.

Bass player Jimmy Garrison called, suggesting we form a trio. At the time I had only one booking ahead—two weeks at the Jazz Workshop in San Francisco—and no group. I said, Fine, let's try it. We can start in San Francisco. Following the Workshop gig we went to see a booking agent who Jimmy thought could line us up with more work. On our way into his office we passed a funny cat coming out in an olive trench coat, carrying a black case. The booker said he was an IRS agent questioning a $2,000 entertainment deduction for which there were no receipts. "I told him whores aren't in the habit of writing out receipts. He went for it . . . I can give you guys two weeks in Boston, three at the Vanguard in New York and maybe a spot on a talk show." Might as well take it, I thought, better than sitting around watching the leaves drop into the swimming pool. Here I go again, back to the big town.

I knew there'd be trouble getting a cabaret card in New York, but I thought I might slip in and out unnoticed, cool it in my funny suit and tie and a shine on my shoes. We made it through a week at the Vanguard, then the management said the police were jamming them and I had to get the card. Appeared before the State Alcoholic Beverage Control. They looked over my records—I could see they were impressed—and said, You'll have to send to L.A. and Fort Worth for additional records, get a clean bill of health from a New York doctor, license from the city police, then report to so-and-so for this and that. It would have taken me weeks to gather all that shit; here I was ready to go for a first-quarter field goal and they were knocking down the posts. The only way these cats were going to be swayed was if I suddenly showed up with Clarence Darrow and $20,000 under the table. I went back and told Jimmy it was no use and caught the next flight home.

22

Watts Burning

The clubs were beginning to hurt. The kids were jamming the rock halls and the older people were staying home watching TV. Maybe they found they couldn't pat their feet to our music anymore. Big-drawing names like Miles and John Coltrane were breaking out of the thirty-two-bar chord-oriented structure and into free expression—or "avant-garde" or "outside," whatever tag you want to stick on it—charging the owners so much they had to raise the covers and minimums. The players who were ace sight readers (which didn't include me) were going into the studios. In the late forties and fifties our music was called "bebop" or "cool jazz" or "funk," and we were neatly tucked into one of those compartments. I don't know why the people who write about music feel they have to slap labels on everything. It's the same watermelon mentality that says niggers can fuck and play boogie-woogie better than whites, Jews are rich, Irish are drunkards, Germans are mean, Japanese are mysterious, and Chinese smoke opium. Who cares? There are only two kinds of music —good and bad. The worst thing that can happen to old good music is that it might become dated for a while, but

138

watch out, in ten to twenty years it will come drifting back like bell-bottoms and W. C. Fields movies. A critic once wrote that I was "the key figure in the current crisis surrounding the funky school of jazz piano." Shit, there wasn't no crisis. All he meant was that I can get down and I can swing. And if he could have looked deep into my life he would have learned that the reason I play the way I do is that I'm taking the years of being pushed off laps, denied love and holding in my natural instincts when I was a kid, of listening to the beautiful spirituals in my father's church and going in the back doors of clubs to play for white audiences, of getting strung and burned in the streets and locked up in dungeons when I tried to find my way—taking all that natural bitterness and suppressed animal feeling out on the piano. That's why I can swing. There really ain't no secret.

When I first heard the new sounds and saw those young kids—most of them not able to do much more than twirl some dials, look weird and play a few stereotyped licks or some far-out unmusical shit that if you ask them what they're doing they say, "Well, I'm out there"—saw them making $15–$20,000 a concert while turning your brains to jelly with the volume, I thought along with the other cats I came up with, How dare they steal my stuff, play it so bad and make all that bread? Running up my banners just the way the older musicians did when Bird got all that fame and glory in the forties. But we all pick up from the players who came before us. In a way I was making the same mistake the critics make: sticking labels on music, putting down a particular style of playing, instead of just judging it good music or bad.

✿   ✿   ✿

It was the summer of 1965. I was working Mitchell's Studio Club, getting a good thing going with Red Mitchell (no relation) on bass and Donald Bailey on drums (one of those reassuring gigs where everything works, acoustics just right, the audience responsive and enjoying itself—proof that you don't necessarily have to turn handsprings or run chimps on roller skates into the act to attract attention) when some brothers decided to tear it up along 103rd, Rosecrans, and surrounding blocks.

I was coming home late from a party in Hollywood after the gig, wheeling down Harbor Freeway, when off to the left I saw what at first looked like a heavy blanket of fog till I noticed the flames spurting through. Decided I'd get off and check it out. I took the Gage Avenue exit and a little while later said to myself, Either a couple of 707's have collided and crashed or else a war has started. Whole blocks were crackling with flames. Must have been the way Rome looked back then, except that these citizens were all a funny color and none of them were wearing togas . . . Never saw so many people on the street at one time in my life—and this is five in the morning. Old people, little people, fat people, kids—looked like they'd just come swarming up out of the ground, waving torches and pistols, firing stores, carrying stuff out, cars screeching up to corners, picking up cats and shooting off again, and the police with their guns standing around at a kind of lazy, bewildered parade rest: shit, can't shoot a whole community. Didn't take me long to check things out and decide to get my ass home before the bazookas and armored trucks arrived. I made it back to the freeway—some nervous firemen trying to direct me the wrong way down one-way streets—shot home and told Jackie, "Watts just declared war on the city of

Los Angeles, and as many motherfuckers as I saw out there tonight they may win."

Next day I called Sonny Criss who lived at 103rd and Central, in the heart of it, and asked him what happened. He said, "I took a fifth of whiskey out to my lawn, sat down and started drinking and laughing. Felt like Nero. Wanted to get out my horn and blow. When I finished the bottle it was dawn, everything was down to the ground and smoking like when you were a kid watching the mist come off a lake."

We didn't go to work the next two nights. No point trying to drive anywhere with the National Guard moving in their armor and brothers firing from the overpasses. I'd missed one Korea and wasn't looking to voluntarily involve myself in another.

The funny thing was that the town grew at the same time it was burning down. It had been a fairly small and compact area as southern California towns go, but after that week everyplace where there had been flames and fighting, from Central to Crenshaw, became Watts.

I wondered what the cats at Fort Worth who used to call me Watts thought when the shit hit the papers. *Hampton said there were some bad motherfuckers around there but not bad enough to burn the place down.*

Watts changed a lot of things. You don't see as many revolving red lights along Central Avenue as you used to. Slap a person around often enough one day he's going to slap back, so you think: Damn, that hurt, better try something different. Niggers have been fucked over for two hundred years and finally some ofays are beginning to feel nervous and guilty. But the only ones who should feel guilty are the ones who fucked over us, not the young girls today who were taught fear of niggers 'cause their mamas might have got raped by a nigger, or *said* she was raped, and the nigger got hung. What we got to remember is to be militant against ignorance, not race, get the shit on right, because the day might come when blacks will no longer be able to use the color they came into the world with as a badge of injustice or a crutch to lean on and help them get ahead. And that's the thing niggers got to watch out for.

Reading the aftermath in the papers, the ruin and desolation, dried blood mixing with the ashes in the streets, I thought of another day in Watts ten years earlier. A hot, sunny summer day on Central Avenue, Bird and Miles and me sitting on the hood of Chuck Thompson's old Deusenberg, while Chuck—who I'd last seen in a white bathrobe in a Rochester, New York hospital ward—squatted in the street shooting pictures of us eating watermelon, trying to look funny.

23

Lillian 527-1083

I suppose I have reason to be bitter. Brought up in ignorance, locked pianos, strung out and tore up, all those stockades and dungeons, Yokohama and back under the gun, ten-year sentence for trying to figure out my life. At least Eldridge Cleaver went to jail for raping a bitch. I don't know who she was but I hope it was good 'cause otherwise it was a damn dumb thing to do. He quivered and got his ass kicked; I got mine kicked for nothing more than sticking a needle in my arm. They snatched me out of the game in the prime of my life, those years when your artistic energy and money-making powers are supposed to be at their peak.

I got to the point once where I thought making money was immoral. Do it for art, for truth, don't sell out, money is evil. Shit. I want to be rich and truthful. I want to be rich and soulful. I want to be rich and honest. I don't want nobody bearing me to the grave like they did poor Clifford and Wardell and Sonny,* saying, Well, he didn't make it, but he sure was beautiful. I want them to say he was a *rich* motherfucker who was beautiful, a good cat who was beautiful. I want to get my due

* Clifford Brown, Wardell Gray, Sonny Clark.

143

this side of the grave, get it without selling out and in time to enjoy it. I don't want to be no casualty on the road to truth.

I want to make music so beautiful it's like hugging in the forest at night, rise to the occasion and maybe go right over it 'cause my energy's burning—and I can make it with nothing but my brains and my hands and my heart. And when that stops beating I'll know I pressed it to the limit and be ready to go down happy.

If our music wasn't dead it was at best a sleeping giant. Many of the brothers who had been the keepers of the flame, the kings of the forties and fifties—all the work they wanted, playing on each other's gigs and recording dates, the young cats all looking up to them—were bitter, brooding about the past green times, hating the kids for taking the bread from their mouths and stealing their glory.

The Mitchell's Studio Club gig had folded, the management turning away from a jazz policy as so many other club owners were doing. I had the feeling it was the final act, the last gig of its kind—the straight-ahead improvising jobs where you could stretch out and burn all night. Other pianists were drifting into the cocktail lounges and the weeks were passing by, empty and aimless. A few offers came in—a funny lounge, backing a rock singer—but I figured I'd struggled this long I wasn't going to succumb now.

A booking agent who had heard me at the Jazz Workshop told a San Francisco real estate man called Dave about me. This Dave had a bar up there called Plain Dave's, which was a deceptive name. What it was was one of those stockbroker-secretary pick-up saloons that the people in San Francisco call body shops or meat markets: maroon leather, polished wood and a lot of mirrors. Dave wanted me to play his place from 5 to 9 five nights a week solo. I wasn't really interested and said to the agent, Tell the motherfucker I want $400. To my surprise he went for it. It was the kind of gig I had been trying to avoid, but there was nothing else in sight and anytime a jazz musician makes $400 a week and carte blanche on food and booze you've got to consider it a good gig.

I wandered in that first afternoon and the bartender said, How you doin', Hamp? It took me a minute to recognize Ray Bass, who I'd last seen in Tokyo in 1954 when I jumped out of his second-story office window with his camera around my neck. The entertainment business has a lot of funny angles and you never know who you're going to run into.

Dave didn't know much about music, but he knew I had a reputation in the field and would often stand by the piano with all the chatter and glasses clinking in the background and call out in his high voice, "Go, Hamp, go." It didn't take me long to peek his game: He was playing Humphrey Bogart to my Play It Again, Sam. End of the first week he said to me, "Not only do you play great, Hamp, but you're a gentleman and a scholar." I thought, I hope this motherfucker don't think I'm a Uncle Tom, and told him not to consider me out of context. He seemed to have an unlimited supply of bread and would shoot at a chick Friday night, ask her if she wanted to have breakfast in Paris in the morning, and when the chick called his bluff, follow through on it. Stop off in London to have some suits made and be back by Monday. Though these bitches' main claim to fame may have been bringing the boss coffee in a Styrofoam cup three times a day, they were his Lauren Bacalls. He'd come in Monday night and say, "Guess where I had breakfast yesterday, Hamp—

Paris." I'd put him on, saying "You mean Pares by Riverside?"
"France." "Goddamn," I'd say, "that must be good pussy."
He'd say, "Not bad. How do you like the suit? Had it made to
order in London, same place where the guy goes who plays
James Bond." And those threads always looked like you could
get them for $95 up on Broadway, next to the topless joints.

Every now and then a lady would send a note over to me:
*I have a piano that hasn't been played in 3 years. Lillian 527-
1083.* Now outside of Ray Bass I was the only black thing in
the place and the only cat not wearing a three-piece suit, so
maybe I looked intriguing to her. Probably telling herself:
Funny cat just sitting there playing the piano, not saying anything. Nothing else going tonight, I'll get way out, fuck a nigger. (Heard it's in, like wearing a snakeskin bracelet or gold-
bug earrings.) But I wasn't in the mood to cat or run any
Super Fly numbers, reap the benefits off the piano like those
cats stepping out with saxophone straps around their necks to
look hip. If I'm going to try to be hip and score, I want to do
it without using the piano as a lure.

It was kind of sad watching those frustrated dudes, most of
them married, come in from the stock exchange every afternoon, lay their tens and twenties out on the bar, look slick and
try to score a broad. I kept my head together by looking at the
gig as a challenge: See if I could capture their attention for a
minute, reach people who would no more think of going inside a jazz club than of stopping to listen to a bird sing in a
tree or milking a cow at dawn. Played all the new, pretty bal-
lads and might as well have been playing to the freaks in the
Ringling sideshow. It got so depressing—Dave alongside me
calling, "Go, Hamp, go"—I'd spend my intermissions standing

out in the alley and at nine o'clock have my nightcap and split fast.

One night a Mexican cat in a green suit strolled in. It took me less than a minute to recognize Vince, the federal agent who had busted me ten years ago after I'd brought him three cents worth of baking soda and charged him $300. Heard I was in town, he said, wanted to hear me play. I looked him straight in the eye and said, "What you doin' these days?" He said, "Working for the water and power company." I said, "Well, I'm glad you're finally turnin' shit on instead of turnin' it off."

I was getting more and more drugged, wondering how much longer I could last at Dave's, when I read that Miles was coming into the Both/And Club. I went down there opening night; Miles looked at me in my sharp suit and said, "Where you playin'?" figuring at 9:30 I must be going to work instead of coming. I told him about my sad gig and sat down to listen. I hadn't played with a group for so long and the music sounded so good to me, I wound up in the middle of a tune with Miles' band wondering, what the fuck am I doing up here. Finished the tune and afterwards asked Miles, "Was it cool?" He said, "You're a crazy motherfucker. It was beautiful." He and Herbie Hancock, the pianist, understood they had made me feel so good again that I just needed a little taste.

It wasn't long after that that my sister Margurite called from L.A. Now Margurite is a straight-ahead, unemotional, together person, and when she calls me long distance I know it's serious. She said, "Hampton—" and I must have had a premonition, I knew what she was going to tell me—"Mama passed this morning."

I caught a midnight flight from Oakland. There had been

a Norman Granz concert in town that night and Duke Ellington, Ella Fitzgerald, and all those top people were on the plane. I thought: All this heavy talent bringing good music to people around the country, they shouldn't have to buy tickets, they should be making as much bread as the Beatles and *own* the damn plane. I'd never met Duke before, and even with thoughts of my mother creeping over me like a shadow I went up to him and said, "I've always wanted to meet you, I'm Hampton Hawes." He looked at me in that warm kingly way he has, eyes twinkling, and said, "Hampton Hawes—I'm aware of you." Made me feel good on this sad trip home.

24

Roses

A lot of brothers—Kenny Clarke, Dexter Gordon, Arthur Taylor—had gone to Europe to play and live. I knew all the arguments: no discrimination, plenty of work; respect and recognition. Why put up with hostility and hard times the rest of your days? We're only going to be here but twenty minutes, better to get your due now rather than fifty years later—some dude in space goggles listening to your records, saying, "That cat really got down, swung his ass off"—while the gardener's pruning the flowers on your grave and the worms inching their way through what's left of you.

Jackie and I had talked about going to Europe, but I had always put the idea off, hoping one day I'd be invited to play there. She was tired of working. It hadn't been much of a marriage over the past couple of years; we were both just hanging on, hoping a miracle would happen. I thought of all the goals I'd set for myself, the things I'd meant to do (buy my mother a grand piano and a house, went to the joint for five years instead), and knew it was time to put some kind of show on the road or it was going to be too late. There was nothing for me to stay home for now; gigs as Play It Again, Sam in San Francisco meat markets weren't an important part of my future. Jackie said she would take a year's sabbatical from school. I could probably hustle some work in Europe and I thought that if we went to a strange place together we might stop drawing apart, maybe she would have to depend on me for a change and I could get into the role I ought to be playing. Home gets to be a drag, try the world.

I was hoping people had heard of me in Europe, that some of my albums had filtered across as they had to Japan in 1954, but I wasn't hoping *too* much, you dig. Didn't want to set myself up for a fall. The reverse number I did on my head ran like this: if I got over there and found no one knew my music, I wouldn't be too drugged; but if it turned out they *had* heard of me, I could enjoy the recognition all the more.

Jackie had submitted her itinerary to the school department and would be getting half pay for studying teaching methods in the various cities. When I looked at the string of tickets, London, Oslo, Copenhagen, Stockholm, Paris, Berlin, Hong Kong . . . I thought, If nothing happens for me musically I'm going to sure get myself some culture.

We weren't in London two hours before we got in a fight: something about money—my bringing a bottle of vodka instead of British beer back to the hotel—so even with good intentions on both sides I could see it was unlikely the shit was ever going to change.

After three weeks in Europe I had worked only one gig, substituting for Vi Redd's pianist a couple of nights at Ronnie Scott's Club in London. I was getting tired of watching other cats play, following Jackie around, arguing. In Copenhagen someone gave us the name of Randy Hultin, a jazz writer for *Down Beat* in Oslo, which was our next stop. We wrote to her, not expecting an answer. But she knew of me and wrote back, Come stay with me in Oslo, I'm sure I can get you work. At the airport she gave us instructions by phone: Take a cab, the door will be open, walk in and make yourselves comfortable; refrigerator's full, help yourself, I'll see you at five. I thought, Damn, these people over here sure do trust each other. Imagine saying walk right in the door's open to someone in L.A. or New York. We found the address and sure enough the door was open. Walked in and the first thing I saw was a big picture of Bud Powell, a red rose in a vase on the table beside him, and another of Bird. I said to Jackie, We came all the way to Norway, but we're home, look at these motherfuckers on the wall. Randy came home at five, said she was very happy to meet me, delighted I was staying in her house, honored. Said, Your picture will be in the papers tomorrow. I said, But I just got off the plane. She said, It's already fixed.

The next day my picture appeared and things started happening. It was like the time you were a kid and touched the punk to the string of firecrackers and they went off so beautifully all in a row. Before the smoke had cleared I was playing in Oslo, Stockholm, Madrid, Berlin—everybody was in Berlin, Dexter, Gordon, Monk, Erroll Garner, half the brothers in the United States seemed to be in Berlin, and we had ourselves a good session and reunion—recording for Radio Norway, Radio Sweden, Radio Denmark, cats paying me $100 just to interview me on the radio. Randy set up more contacts and I'd find people meeting the plane when I came down in a new city, lines forming outside the clubs—quiet as a church in a forest when I played—recording companies asking me to record albums with their players. Made me feel important. The reverse number I'd done on my head had worked almost too well—I could hardly believe what was happening. Music to these people was like the stock market and football in America.

Though Jackie and I had some difficulties with the different languages—ordering meals or buying cigarettes—there was never any problem communicating with the musicians. Music has its own language. We were like boats flying different flags crossing the Mediterranean, communicating in a friendly fashion by semaphore, trading stories, throwing lifelines across if we got close enough; but there weren't going to be any hassles unless we started shooting across each other's bows.

From Barcelona, where we were evicted from our hotel because some people from the club followed me and Jackie home and tried to crowd into our room—never been evicted under groovier circumstances and I told the manager, "Shit man, you people really take your music seriously over here"—we caught a train to Paris. Lester Koenig had told me to get in touch with Jean Louis Ginibre in Paris because he had written some pieces about me in the French *Jazz* Magazine. He and his wife Simone, who booked American musicians in Europe, took Jackie and me to dinner at a fine restaurant on the Champs Élysées and asked what my plans were. I told them Jackie was on her sabbatical, and I was here to play if I could. They said, We can easily fix that for you. I said, Please fix it.

They arranged a concert, TV and radio shows, and a steady gig at the Cameleon, a little club on the left bank. No sooner had I settled in there than Kenny Clarke called, asking me to fly to Rome for a concert. Now the only musician I knew who might be able to sub for me at the Cameleon was the Swiss pianist George Gruntz, who had come to hear me play on one of my earlier stops. Two years before he had come to California to appear at the Monterey Jazz Festival. The Festival people had flown him 8,000 miles to play a concert 300 miles north of L.A., and I had never even received as much as a brochure from them! I reached him at his home; he said he wasn't doing anything, would be glad to help me out, and drove down from Switzerland the next day.

I left Jackie in Paris—Italy was coming up on our itinerary anyway—and caught a flight to Rome. The concert with Kenny, Johnny Griffin and Jimmy Woode was a big success. It was probably the first time in a long while those people had seen four brothers from the States playing together; usually one American would be featured, backed by local players. They threw roses on the bandstand, gave us a big banquet afterwards. A second concert was lined up for us in Pascara. More roses, another big dinner, trips to villas and castles. I caught myself having a better time when I wasn't with Jackie, wishing I had come to Europe on my own. Began to feel funny about it and tried to put it in the back of my mind, but when I returned to Paris Jackie sensed the change and we grew more distant and uneasy with each other. She would flare up every now and then even though I thought I was making things bearable—we had a long way to go on this trip yet—but there was a kind of momentum working, something pushing us farther apart each day.

I thanked George Gruntz for subbing for me and before splitting back to the Alps he said, "If you ever come to Switzerland, you'll never have to worry about a job." (That raised an echo in my mind, and I remembered what the Ringling Brothers road manager had told me after the Fort Worth show: If you ever need a gig when you get out, give me a ring.)

One night Jean Louis Ginibre brought the French pianist

and composer Martial Solal into the Cameleon. I had heard Martial's records; his fire and technique and imagination were so heavy he was considered the Art Tatum of France. The only difference was he couldn't get a gig in his hometown, while the American expatriate musicians were jamming those clubs! Martial's sin was that he had become "local" and was taken for granted in Paris like I was in L.A., had to leave the country or go to a town like Nice to get a gig. Jean Louis suggested we record together. I told him there should be a statue of this motherfucker on the Champs Élysées, he can play like six piano players, he doesn't need me. But Martial said, Hamp, we both hit the door and it didn't bust. Let's hit it together and maybe it will give. We rehearsed for a week, grooved together, and cut an album backed by Kenny Clarke on drums and a French bass player. Jean Louis was so excited over the results he had his wife Simone book us as a two-piano trio on a string of concerts in France, Belgium and Italy. It was a beautiful time.

I could understand why so many musicians who had come over here had never gone back, but I wondered how happy they were. When I met brothers I'd known in the States the first thing they said was, "They built a new freeway, huh?" . . . "Shelly's still going?" "What happenin' on Central?" In Amsterdam I saw Don Byas, one of the greatest tenor players in the world; motherfucker's roots go so deep if saxophones were trees he'd be a redwood. He'd been living over there so long he started talking to me in French, then German; when he finally switched to English I still couldn't understand him. I thought, What are beautiful cats like this doing in European capitals? They should be back blowing at Shelly's and the Half Note close to the source where the music was changing and evolving—things happening that might not reach Europe for years. If they stayed over here much longer they were in danger of becoming local like Martial Solal. No need to travel 8,000 miles for that. Shit, if I'm going to be local, let me be local at 35th and Budlong where I was born and raised. Sure, blacks are treated better in Europe, but that could be because the Europeans haven't become indoctrinated yet, haven't had us on their backs and consciences for two hundred years. Maybe half the people are treating us nice because we're American so we must have a lot of bread to spend, and the other half because we're *black* Americans and they want to be hip, dissociate themselves from the peckerwoods back home. Well if that's the case, I don't need that kind of life just so I can work more often, drive on the left side of the road and walk free down a boulevard with a blonde bitch on my arm. I'd rather face the shit at home—at least most of that is sincere.

Martial and I had more concerts in Spain, but Jackie's schedule said we had to move on. I resented having to cut short my tour, but I couldn't let her go on alone. You make a commitment to someone, you got to follow through. I said to Martial, I've had fun, I wish I could make those other gigs, but I got to go.

We had stayed so long in Paris our Euro-Rail pass ran out and we had to buy new fares for Rome and Athens. Our second morning in Athens I came downstairs and the hotel manager was holding a newspaper with big headlines over his head, shouting across the lobby to me, "They have killed your leader." For a second, before I focused on the print, I thought this cat had got hold of a five-year-old paper. When we reached Tel Aviv a few days later we saw Martin Luther King's picture hanging in a black frame on the wall of the American Embassy. Flags at half-mast and black marines standing guard out front.

In Jerusalem, witnessing all the different crosses and temples and mosques, I thought of my mother dying and my father talking about God and how he had once drilled some of the congregation with rifles after prayer meeting because threats had been coming into the church. I couldn't believe how alike the Arabs and Jews looked. The only way to tell them apart was to check which side wore the burnooses. They shared the same dry land, the hot sun had burned the same color into them, so why the fuck were they always killing each other?

Bombay turned me around. I'd never seen poverty before. Been hungry in the streets of New York, a junkie, been in jail, but I've never seen anybody as fucked up and pitiful as those people in India. It blew my mind to see babies with bloated bellies, women washing them in the streets from fire hydrants, old ladies and cats with crooked arms from malnutrition coming up to you begging for pennies. Makes you stop and take stock. Here I was thinking about making a big splash, a hit record, going home a hero, and I'm walking the streets with motherfuckers who don't even know what a piece of bread is, let alone Stravinsky or Charlie Parker. If Bird came alive and played for them they wouldn't be able to hear him because they'd be too damn hungry. It tore my mind away from music and the good things that had been happening to me in Europe, from Jackie and myself. I was just one motherfucker trying to make it, but here were millions trying to make it on a simpler level—fighting for a piece of bread—and a whole lot of them weren't doing so good. Made me think I had no right to be worrying about how much my next gig would pay, how cool it would be, maybe I ought to consider myself lucky just making a living as well as anyone else so I can eat and pay my bills and have a house and be with people I love, do my gig and die and get on out of here, maybe that's all I got a right to expect.

In Tokyo, still trying to leave India behind—and China, more of the same, people living out their whole lives on little junks in the bay—we hadn't been in our hotel but one hour when the press came pouring into our room. The only thing I could figure was someone must have recognized me in the lobby. When we left the hotel to take a walk photographers started following us, buzzing around, shooting pictures. I thought, What the hell's happening, do they think I'm the new black Secretary of State? I knew some of my albums had been released here, and I'd done a lot of playing around Tokyo and Yokohama, but that was fourteen years ago. The Hilton management figured I must be somebody, got nervous and sent their public relations man up to our room. He took us to dinner, had his picture taken with me, and *still* didn't know who I was.

RCA Victor called the next day, said they wanted me to record. Director Masaaki Hisamatsu suggested I do a solo album, something I'd always wanted to try. Recorded a dozen tracks over three sessions, called it "The Challenge," and was resting up from that encounter when Columbia phoned, asking if I'd like to do an album with some of the local musicians I'd played with in the fifties. I thought, Ain't this a bitch: two albums, RCA and Columbia, in one week and I can't even tell you what street either company is on in Hollywood!

The Columbia session was set up with a live audience to capture a jam-session atmosphere. When Sleepy Matsumoto,

George Ohtsuka and the other musicians who I hadn't seen in fourteen years walked into the studio they greeted me with open arms and one word: "Uma-san!" We didn't bother with arrangements, just jammed the same tunes we'd played all those years ago at Ray Bass' Harlem Club and the Tennessee Coffee Shop—except for one original which I called "Uma-San's Blues." It was a groovy session and a warm reunion with my brothers.

Just as we were getting ready to leave Tokyo the U.S. Air Force sent a cat to the hotel to ask if I would play a concert for the men. Well, here I was 6,000 miles from home and even with the memory of various stockades, the cement dungeon with the clanking doors, alive in my mind I guess I still felt something for the flag. They sent a big black limousine for me, and riding in the back seat beside an old Smilin' Jack with silver birds on his shoulders I couldn't help thinking of that other Far East trip, scrunched between the MP's in the little Japanese sedan that had taken me to the Big 8.

Our final week in Japan I rented a car and drove to Camp Drake and Asaka—trying to recapture my King Farouk days in the whorehouse and the times walking fire guard, my family keeping me company on the other side of the f nce. The camp was still there, but I hardly recognized the town: new buildings and gas stations, the river covered over to make a freeway; even the trees and rice paddies on the outside of town looked funny. I couldn't orient myself; it was like being in a town you vaguely remember passing through a long time ago on the way to somewhere else. When I finally located the spot where Mama-san's house had stood I found a strange little building with a sign out front, HOTEL SUNSHINE, and a ground floor stand-up counter selling hot dogs, chili and Cokes.

I was looking forward to getting home. The trip had given me a big boost; it was like someone considering himself second class all his life and learning it's not necessarily so—the funny-looking red glass might be a ruby. Around the world in one hundred days, gigs in ten countries, lines out front, seven albums in nine months. All on my own. Treated like royalty. In L.A. I couldn't find a straight jazz gig, couldn't get past the studio gates. I've been a member of the L.A. union for twenty-five years, and not once in that time have I ever got a job from them. They should give me a gold card. Instead they keep sending me reminders, "You are $10 in arrears on your work dues." All those beautiful things came down in Europe and Japan because the people in those countries had heard my music, said, Here's an artist from the States, let's record him, give him the recognition and respect that's due him. Wanted me to keep playing, went out of their way to help. The way they received me reinforced my dignity, left me thinking, *I must be important to be treated like that, better take care of myself.*

But all the time those groovy things were going on I kept feeling a pull toward home. You have to go back to the source to listen and grow, you can't ever be satisfied. The States are where it all started, the terminal from where the trains head out in all different directions, some of them lazy little milk runs, some ninety mile-an-hour cannonball expresses. The music was changing so fast now it was already passing the expatriates by, leaving some of them playing 1950's tunes in 1950's styles.

The afternoon we left Tokyo a crazy thing happened. A

Japanese reporter rushed up to me in the airport terminal, said the BBC in London had just reported me killed in a car crash in Switzerland. I said, Well you're about to see a ghost get on a plane for California. Four days after I got home the BBC phoned at five in the morning. I had checked out the local scene, saw no work in sight and was going to the unemployment office that day to start collecting on the Plain Dave's gig. They said, Is this Hampton Hawes? I said, Yeah, you woke me up. They said, We're trying to confirm your death last week in a motor accident outside Geneva. I said, I'm alive and broke in Los Angeles. Hung up and said to Jackie, Ain't that a bitch, a motherfucker got to die to get some publicity.

25

Blue Strings

I should have known that my Europe-Orient triumph wasn't going to open up anything for me at home. Martial Solal's stateside trip hadn't done shit for him in Paris. Two months went by and the only work I got worth taking was a couple of weekends at Shelly's. I'd run across the cats working the studios and they'd apologize to me for what they were doing. Shit, no need to apologize. Only wish I'd had the right training when I was coming up and taken advantage of the breaks instead of messing up. Here I was back from my heavy trip, new lease on life, I thought, and I was out hustling work in the streets like I was twenty again and had not even begun to pay my dues. Feeling sorry for myself because in another two months I was going to be forty years old and it was beginning to look like I just might not ever make it.

I was sitting around the swimming pool thinking my gloomy thoughts when Harvey Siders, a correspondent for *Down Beat*, phoned to ask for an interview about my European experiences. I agreed and during the course of the taping he put one of those "What would you do if" questions interviewers like to ask: What would I do if I suddenly had a new manager, a recording contract, a good A and R man and a chance to make a record that was slightly commercial? Given the existing conditions, would I compromise when it came to that moment of truth? I remembered the time Les Koenig at Contemporary had given me a batch of soul tunes that people like Ramsey Lewis and Les McCann had had hits with. I took them home, tried them out, went back to Les and said, I can't do it, I can't go against what I feel. The conditions were pretty much the same then as now. I answered Harvey, "If they gave me junk to play I'd probably tell them to kiss my ass and walk out—then wake up the next morning and say to myself, You're a damn idiot."

A week later the fantasy came true. Jack Lewerke and Ralph Kaffel of Vault Records got the idea that I should record an album with strings featuring tunes from movie musicals like *Oliver* and *Funny Girl*. Now there are some pretty tunes from those shows and the strings would all be pearl studio musicians from the MGM Orchestra, so it wasn't as if I was going over to the other side, joining Lawrence Welk's Siamese piano team or working a tea in the Pink Room. Nat Cole, André Previn and other cats had had success with the format, and the Vault people thought my style and attack would present a good contrast to the fiddles. I thought, Nothing else going on, it might be fun; I'll give an inch and see what happens. They gave me the scores to all the shows, from which I picked the ones I thought I could best groove on, and hired Billy Byers, an arranger-conductor-trombonist I'd known since the forties, to conduct and help me write the charts.

Billy's a big success in his field, lives in a Malibu house that looks bourgeois from the outside, but inside it's like a giant playpen, scribbling all over the walls, cute little Japanese wife, and a raft of funny kids flying around. I'd take my ideas over to his place and we'd work the stuff out. He's been at his game so long, has his shit down so cold, he could write out those lush charts with one hand and be eating a ham sandwich with the other while the kids went scrambling around the room and his wife wandered in and out in her bathing suit. . . . "What if we change the time signature here?" . . . "Oh, you'd like an augmented passage there? Beautiful . . ." Note it down and be biting into his sandwich and digesting the motherfucker while a kid went somersaulting over his feet.

The day of the session he introduced me to the strings: "Ladies and gentlemen, our performer this afternoon is Mr. Hampton Hawes." Cool. Made me feel like I should be wearing a bow tie, spats, and a green velvet coat; wished I'd taken more time combing my hair. They all nodded at me and I nodded back. Had to check myself to keep from bowing from the waist. When the cat in the number one chair looked at me extra long I figured he must be someone heavy like the concertmaster, so I gave him an extra nod.

Billy handed me some earphones, passed out the music and we got under way. Every now and then I'd peek over my shoulder at the rows of arms bent just so, the fat cellos, the big violins and little ones all sawing away like a small wheat field waving in the wind, sight reading that shit like it was a second-grade storybook. Between takes of "How are Things in Glocca Morra?" a stubby-legged little chick on one of the cellos complained she was getting tired playing the same pedal note for so many bars. I felt sorry for her and suggested we change the note to a moving line but Billy told me not to worry, it was just an everyday flash of temperament, that she was a pro and if necessary could keep sawing away on that one note all day long.

For the first couple of tracks the atmosphere put me uptight, forced me to be extra careful and precise on the cues: afraid they'd be wondering, Who's this peasant we're playing with? Laying out during orchestral passages I had to fight an urge to check my shoelaces, stand up and comb my hair. After a while I loosened up, told myself the precision, bending to the fiddles, wasn't all that important and I'd be better off feeling the entrances, going my natural way. The stuff sure sounded pretty. If it hadn't been for the jazz rhythm section and the earphones sliding off my head whenever I looked up to peek at the strings or catch a cue from Billy, I would have felt like André Watts or Carmen Cavallaro playing a concert with Kostelanetz at the Hollywood Bowl.

When the session was over the strings came up to me and each one shook my hand; said, "Nice to have played with you, Mr. Hawes, we enjoyed it." Then Billy dismissed them and we listened to the playbacks. He'd voiced those fiddles so good, they sounded like a damn philharmonic.

The album was released under the title "Blue Strings," but nothing much happened with it. The week it came out I turned forty.

26

Watts and White Fence

I've sometimes thought that marriage is like having your own group. If the fire and freshness and sincerity are there and you don't run out of ideas, you can stay together forever. But when those things start fading, when you're no longer sending signals and playing off each other's ideas—no matter how many gigs you got lined up ahead, it's time to split.

The stage wasn't set until the summer of 1971 when Jack Lewerke of Vault Records sponsored me for the Montreux Jazz Festival in Switzerland and Simone Ginibre called from Paris to say she could supply other European dates around it. Simone asked what kind of money I had in mind. Well, the times I haven't been in demand—which generally covers the period since 1963 when I came back from five years' exile—I've tried not to low-rate my market price because once your meat is down, they'll always try to buy it cheaper. I said, I know what I'm worth, but I don't know how much I can get. Just don't embarrass me.

I'd been in Europe about three weeks when I decided to send for Jackie. The past year she'd let me know that although I was supposed to be the heavy talent in the house, she had

165

paid as much in taxes as I had earned. I wanted to prove I could not only provide for her, but give her a trip to Europe on me—didn't want her thinking that when things started going good I was going to be jive and forget about the times she helped me. But most of all I wanted to give our life together one more chance; if there was anything I could do to save it, I wanted to try.

Just before I sent for Jackie, my bass player Henry Franklin got lonely for his girl Penny and cabled her to come over. There was a lot weighing on my mind. We had come to Europe on a 45-day excursion fare and other offers had come in which would take us past the deadline. On top of that, Jackie was due to arrive in a week.

Penny showed up with a friend, Josie Black, a beautiful Mexican-Indian chick with long black hair and rings on most of her fingers. I had met her with Jackie at the going-away party for the trio at Henry's pad in L.A. a month ago. She had been on my mind ever since. I think if you've been through a lot of turmoil in your life, you're naturally drawn to someone who's been through some shit of their own.

We all had rooms in the same hotel. Henry and I showed Penny and Josie around town—Champs Élysées, Eiffel Tower, the Louvre—cautioning them to be careful crossing the streets because Paris traffic is worse than in any American city, they'll run over you in a minute. Josie and I must have fallen in love in that short week without even realizing it or thinking about it. Not a moonlight or "eyes" attraction, just two minorities, Watts and White Fence,* 6,000 miles from home, trying to figure out what was going on in their lives. Offering each other comfort and solace, walking the boulevards, sometimes not

* Mexican area in East Los Angeles.

even talking, as if we'd known each other a long time. When I learned what she'd been through—her mother locked up in an institution before she was a year old, an upbringing even stricter than mine in the Pentecostal Church (singing and playing the tambourine while her father preached, watching those people fall down and shake), three marriages, the first at fifteen to a cat who killed himself, and a ten-year-old boy, Billy, to raise—when I heard all that shit I was surprised she didn't get strung out like me.

I watched after her, bought her a ring for the one finger that was free (told her, That one's going to be mine), brought her back an ashtray I swiped from the Savoy Grand Hotel in Cortina where we played an overnight concert, a pretty colored china dish with a picture on its base of a winding boulevard and white villas against the Alps. She knew about Jackie, knew I was locked into a twenty-year marriage, and had a sense of loyalty about that. There was no conscious idea of being together when we got back to L.A. Jackie would be arriving in a day or two; it had been a nice week and that would be the end of it. We were two people a long ways from home looking into each other's eyes, saying, Damn, I know what you mean . . . You sick of this shit too? You tired of this merry-go-round? And maybe if we held hands for a little while, it might not be too bad.

Neither of us was prepared for what eventually came down.

Jackie arrived in Paris the first week in August. To avoid complications Josie split with Henry and Penny for London, where they had a friend with a pad; assured me before she left that when we all got together again I didn't have to worry, she wasn't going to be funny, wasn't even going to know me, it'd be cool. I bought two tickets for Portugal and for the next two weeks Jackie and I lay in the sun on the beach at Estoril. With so much on my mind I figured I'd just lay on my back in that fine white sand and try to forget about everything. But all the time I knew the shit was working on me.

When we all met back in London for the Ronnie Scott's gig Jackie immediately knew something was funny; she's smart and can sense those things. Knew it wasn't Penny, and it sure wasn't Henry or Mike, the drummer—all three feeling nervous at this stage, caught in the middle and beginning to realize that the week's fling was in danger of tearing up some lives. They'd even encouraged it at the start, played Cupid, thinking I was jiving, being a hip musician in Paris—tip out on the old lady, little stuff on the side but it'll pass over in a minute—not dreaming the shit could get out of hand. I'd had one or two girls before, but Jackie knew where my head was at, knew I was loyal and wasn't going nowhere; that I couldn't jive for any length of time and still be at peace with myself. But this time she sensed something a little heavier going on.

During our first week at Ronnie Scott's club in London a brother who had played Sporting Life in *Porgy and Bess* threw a party for the trio at his pad; we had met him earlier in the tour and he and his wife had followed us around on various European gigs. Tension had been building in our group and Jackie didn't feel up to going. I went alone, decided it wasn't right she shouldn't be there, went back to the hotel with Henry and Mike and talked her into coming.

With Jackie on one side of the room, Josie on the other, I started drinking and a lot of things went whirring through my mind . . . Twenty years. Sevener married us in his study, said to love, honor and obey; drummed loyalty and decency into me. This is your wife, stick with her, do right and take care of her till the day you die. She took pride in my career, kept a scrapbook, did what she thought was best for me; stuck by me all those years I was strung and didn't disown me . . . Then not looking to do anything but take care of business, something beautiful drops into my life on the Champs Élysées. Knew it was real, she couldn't be after my fame or money, ex-junkie can't get a decent gig in his own home town, won't find my albums on any charts or my name on posters at Carnegie Hall. Wished I could have charmed her with four trips around the world instead of tiptoeing around hotel corridors, tearing my damn self up with worrying, trying not to be cruel to anyone. (Could probably have handled it if I'd been brought up in the Muslim religion which says you can have as many bitches as you want, legally.) I've never dug chippying, playing hip games. Once went with a young blond bitch, looked like a Swedish starlet and it was like having a Hertz-Rent-a-Bitch, couldn't even enjoy the pussy. Why should I have one woman for one thing and a different one for another? If it's good, why not the same woman all the time? Here was a chance to change my destiny, just like I'd kicked twelve years ago, taken the reins out of the Man's hands . . . Why should I suffer anymore, been through so many ups and downs and gathered enough credentials along the way, I got as much right as anyone to just lie down, have a note pinned on me—read *Fuck it*—let 'em lay me right in the casket. Historians would look at it, nod, agree he's got a right to that epitaph, all the shit he's been through. (What I'd really like to have them say is, Look at all that cat accomplished and he didn't go through *nothin'*.) . . . Shit, I'd been half dead for twenty years. John Kennedy,

Bird, Martin King in their graves were more alive than I was, might as well be down there with them. They lived their lives full while they were here, said Bye for a while, and their shit is marching on . . .

Drinking hard and thinking all these strange thoughts, I must have snapped, gone on a strange trip; never been on one just like this before, pulling off my clothes in this jiveass room, getting naked. Josie told me later she turned around, saw me in my draws, my shirt off, sitting on the floor unzippering my boots and thought, Well, he's out but he won't go any further. When she next turned around I was stark naked, bowing to people—saw out of the corner of my eye Jackie splitting the room—then stretching out on my back and lighting a cigarette. Delivering what you might call a sermon to the faces peering down: "I don't know why everyone's nervous, going to be worms crawling up everybody's asshole in about twenty minutes . . . Ain't nobody in the world so bad if his heart stops pumping he's not going to be dead. You leave with what you came in with, walk in with two bags, can't say I meant to bring four . . ." The last thing I remember is flicking ashes into somebody's discarded wooden shoe and Jackie bending over me, putting an ashtray by my head.

I don't know why the tension took that form. I wasn't trying to be strange or funny. I was up against a wall, getting crushed, knew I had to do something different to relieve the pressure. When I got down on that floor naked I felt like I had stripped off something ugly, and when I stood up and put my clothes back on I was clean.

At the start of the tour Henry and Mike and I had established a ritual of grabbing each other's hands just before we went on the stand, like a football team leaving the locker room: block out everything extraneous, go out there and give all. By the time we reached the Montmartre Club in Copenhagen that outside shit had intruded and things seemed ready to explode.

Opening night: big crowd, tables almost full. I looked around and saw everybody but the right person. The night before Jackie and I had gone to a party. She had left early and when I got back to the hotel it was after three in the morning. Went straight to Josie's room. I was sick of fighting my own feelings, trying to pacify everyone; mad at myself for getting involved with Josie, for picking the wrong woman twenty years back down the road, juggling the lives of two people I loved and maybe putting a whole lot of hurt on somebody. Josie had told me she'd heard sounds outside her door earlier and thought it might be Jackie checking. I wasn't going to hide any longer; I knew if a knock came on the door I'd open the damn thing and get the shit over with because the vibes were growing stronger and nobody seemed able to control them. I never got the chance. When Josie said a minute later, There it is again . . . I pulled the door open and saw my bathrobe disappearing around the corner.

I looked around the club again—it was time to start the first set—and said to Henry, Where's Josie? He said he didn't think she wanted to come. I split and caught a taxi back to the hotel.

Josie was crying when she opened the door.

"Why didn't you come?"

"They're getting nervous, they didn't want me to."

"Put on your clothes and let's go."

We walked in the club together and I found an empty table

for her. Wide open now, defiant, letting everyone in our group
know I was through jiving. Jackie and Penny were sitting at
a table near the bandstand. As I passed them Jackie surprised
me; said, "What you did was beautiful."

From the piano I watched Penny walk over to Josie's table
and then Josie following her back to where Jackie was sitting.
Josie told me later the following exchange went down:

"You don't have to sit by yourself."

"Okay."

"He's had girl friends before, you're not the first one who's
chased him."

"I'm not chasing him."

"After twenty years he's not going anywhere."

"I'm not trying to take him anywhere."

At the same time Mike's bass drum was sliding and he
stopped in the middle of a tune to drive a damn nail into the
floor. I got up, started to kick one of the drums off the stand,
told Henry to take a solo and walked into the back room.
Thinking some funny thoughts like, The shit's really deterio-
rating . . . Better not do anything far out in this strange town,
they might lock me up. Jackie came back after a minute and
said, "Please, Hamp, cool it."

"Okay."

Two days later, a week before the tour ended, Josie and
Penny had to catch their charter flight from London back to
the States.

27

Receipt

Back home I kept wavering, trying to have it both ways. Torn between Compton—where Jackie and I were like two strangers in a big rooming house, our heads so far apart there were hardly any arguments anymore—and Josie's place, squinting at my watch in the dark to see when the sun would be up and wondering what I'd be confronted with when I got home. Hating to have to lie to Jackie so that most of the time I wouldn't answer when she asked me where I'd been . . . Call Josie to tell her I'd be right over if it seemed a good time to slip out of the house, then start drinking, trying to figure out what lie to use and not show until hours later or not show at all. Phone the next day to apologize and tell her we can bring it off if we hang tough.

I could almost get out of myself and watch Jackie watching *me* tear myself up, wondering, How can he think about leaving a swimming pool and four bedrooms for a shack in the ghetto, start all over again at his age; knowing it wasn't in my nature to do things halfway, play this kind of game. After twenty years she had me figured out, I'd always come back to her

173

before. Then one day, mad, phoning Josie's house and when Josie put me on—*How's your whore doing?*

Josie couldn't handle it much longer. *You can't have it two ways, you're hurting everybody. If you don't make up your mind soon I'm going to run from you.* Her son Billy sensed the trouble: When I'd get in my car after being with his mother I'd find he had locked the wire gate at the foot of the driveway, not wanting me to leave. Kids know what's going down, you can't play 'em cheap.

You going to make up your mind or kill your damn self worrying?

When I finally made my choice, it was the hardest thing I've ever had to do—harder than kicking because I wasn't dealing with a spoon of shit running through my veins but with the feelings of the two people in the world I was closest to. Canceled twenty years of love and loyalty and suffering by walking into Jackie's room one morning and saying, "I've got to go, I'm sorry."

Put my clothes in the car and drove to Josie, found her watering the lawn. Shut off the water, took her by the hand and sat her on our bed.

"Do you want me?"

"Yes."

"You got me."

Left a person I loved for another person I loved. No wonder I got naked in London, tore up in Copenhagen, drunk in L.A. That receipt always comes back to you.

When I broke the news to Sevener he said, "Well, after twenty years I can't say you didn't try. Two people who can't hold hands shouldn't walk together."

28

Magi

The dead years began to slip away. It was like that fresh, early time when I was a kid just learning, heard a tune with some cool changes and thought, Shit, I gotta get that down; got it and it felt good. But the sounds had changed along with the times. A week after moving in with Josie I put on some of my old Bird and Tatum records for her because she'd never been exposed to jazz. I listened through two tracks of the Tatum and took it off. Put on Bird, took him off. Josie thought it was because she wasn't showing enough enthusiasm and asked for another chance. But it wasn't that. The records no longer worked for *me*. Never thought I'd walk away from Bird and Tatum—not that they weren't as great as they'd ever been, but their message was delivered a long time ago and maybe it had been heard too many times since. A fresh, new sound was ripping across the country. I no longer had to listen to dead giants to make me feel good.

Josie Black was like the best shot of shit I ever had, but instead of making me nod it got me off my ass. Drove me up to Berkeley where a new record company, Fantasy-Prestige, had just formed. Cats I'd recorded for before under different labels. I told them, For twenty-five years I've been guarding the fort, but I'm pulling my banners down and putting my armor aside. Going on a new trip. Got my ass kicked with Project X, switching to Y. And those good cats checked out my new plans, my Afro and my funny clothes, and said, Come aboard.

Our cottage is in a section of East L.A. known as White Fence because of the gang by that name who consider it their turf. There haven't been any clashes lately, but sometimes at night the gangs from other neighborhoods will cruise down our street calling softly, "White Fence . . . White Fence," letting the local kids know they're coming through. Gives me a little chill when I hear it, even though the section is not much different from the Watts area where I grew up.

Four little rooms with a lemon tree out back, couple of funny dogs so happy to see me when I drive up in the Camaro they jump up on the hood. You could almost fit the whole cottage into the Compton swimming pool. In the tiny living room is an electric piano and twin speakers the size of *Space Odyssey 2001* slabs. Two new albums on the shelf, all original tracks on which I play three electric keyboards and an Arp Synthesizer that gets a flute sound like a drunk cobra coming out of a green basket in Egypt (but never forgetting to pat my feet). The bathroom is off our bedroom and when her kid Billy has to go he'll come through our room, so it's a cozy arrangement. I never thought much about having a kid of my own and it's probably too late now. I wouldn't have the right attitude or the patience to bring someone up and wouldn't want to do a bad job of it. I guess the older you get the more you worry about your own ass and the more selfish you become about your time; Josie knows I want her with me wherever I go. But I figure I'm ahead of the game: got a son ready-made, didn't have to wait nine months and watch Josie's belly sticking out like a wheelbarrow, saved myself a lot of cigars, and clapping a lot of dudes I might not dig on the back. Billy's twelve and he's beautiful, and it's the same as having my own. I've never understood those cats who won't go with a woman who has a kid because they feel cheated: Want everyone in their family stamped with their personal imprint. For three minutes of someone else's pleasure they got to go on a trip about it. What difference does it make who fucks who, so long as when the kid comes he's loved and respected and treated right? I'm not nervous about my name living after me. My name will go down with me and I'll hope I've served it well and be proud of it. First day of the new school term Billy was given a slip to fill out: Write your mother's and father's name and your address. His father's name is Richard Gallock, he knows that, but what he wrote was: Mother's name *Josie Black*, Father's name *Hampton Hawes*. Didn't know how to spell mine so he copied it off one of the albums. What he was saying was, There are two people giving me love and taking good care of me so they must be my mother and father.

On days when I have musicians over for rehearsals I'll sometimes feel a cool draft on my back, look around and see a row of little heads sticking in the window: Billy's brought his friends over to check out the music. (I taught him "Three Blind Mice" and a few other pieces, and I always know when he's been fucking around the piano because I'll see or feel dirt on the keys. Then I'll have to clean the board and wash my hands before I play again.)

‌ ‌ ‌ ‌ ‌ ❖ ❖ ❖

A lot of shit has gone down in the last two decades. Basin Street and Birdland are dead, the Blackhawk in San Francisco where Lenny Bruce would come in to cow is a parking lot, and you wouldn't recognize Central Avenue; Mr. Konton's, where I turned the autumn leaves blue the week John Kennedy let me out of the dungeon, is now the Blue Angel featuring belly dancers with rhinestones in their navels. All those brothers who went down so fast: Bird, Clifford, Wardell, Tatum, Bud, Billie, Trane . . . the names read like an honor roll plaque in one of those little shady town parks. Seems like they barely lasted through the springtime of their lives, casualties on the road to truth. Not many of us survived; some still strung, trying to get out of the woods, others expatriates, becoming "local" in alien cities. A few of us jumping into electronics, picking up from and sharing with the kids—the critics who once championed us putting us down for trying to find a new road, deserting the tried and true, just as they put down Bird and Dizzy and Monk in the forties. What we may have to do is close ranks just as those cats did. But the styles are coming together, the labels finally loosening and falling away, and one day they'll find they only need to write about good music or bad. (I know if I ever become famous enough to appear on *This Is Your Life* the producers will be in trouble trying to track down my friends; might have to settle for reading the legends on the gravestones in that shady town park.)

A little while ago Josie and I spent our first Christmas together. Woke up Christmas morning to the dogs barking and the tramp of little feet past our window. Looked out and saw a row of funny heads bobbing by: Billy and his friends bearing gifts. Marched right into our room like the Magi, bringing candy bars, oranges and lemons and apples wrapped in colored paper. Took me back a minute to my brother and sisters at 35th and Budlong and to Mama-san and the little kids in the Asaka whorehouse. Here I had another family. I thought of Jackie, hoping she was having as nice a Christmas as mine.